Going to the Dogs

Confessions of a Mobile Pet Groomer

Jan Nieman

Going to the Dogs

Confessions of a Mobile Pet Groomer

Jan Nieman

New Chapter Publisher

Sarasota, Florida 2010

New Chapter Publisher

GOING TO THE DOGS
Confessions of a Mobile Pet Groomer

ISBN 978-0-984-1745-7-7
Copyright © 2010 by Jan Nieman

Published by New Chapter Publisher
  1765 Ringling Blvd.
  Suite 300
  Sarasota, FL 34236
  941-954-4690

Cover design and layout by Shaw Creative
Illustrations by Hyunhee Park

. . . .

Here's to pet lovers
whose actions speak louder than words
when they rescue animals, provide homes,
and donate time and money for the care
of God's special creatures.

. . . .

Dogs are really people with short legs in fur coats.

—Author unknown

 There are no ordinary cats.

—Colette

Contents

· ·

When a dog wags her tail and barks at the same time,
how do you know which end to believe?

—Anonymous

Introduction

I must confess I never would have dreamed that, while trudging through my previous careers, my final one would be as a "mobile pet groomer." I'm not even sure I had ever heard the phrase. However, hidden among my five children was a "doggie-phile" daughter who led me at age forty-five into the thrilling world of dog grooming.

After returning from her first year in college, Kris announced, "Mom and Dad, I don't know what I really want to do. So-o-o, what would you think about sending me to dog grooming school?"

Huh? My husband Niel and I were unaware there *was* such a thing as a school for grooming dogs, but we added up the numbers. With three other children in college, if Kris chose a semester learning how to clean up pets rather than four expensive years in higher education, the winner was...?

Meanwhile, my job at the Social Security Administration wasn't panning out. Dealing with upper management personalities at one end, while supervising employees at the other, was turning me into an indecisive administrator empathizing with everyone's viewpoints. I took advantage of every sick day and planned exotic vacations before actually earning the leave. Another indication I was spiraling downward was the disturbing discovery of clumps of hair on my pillow and in my brush. Was I losing my mind along with my hair?

Clearly, it was time to move on, and Kris' new career sounded quite attractive. I, too, could play with dogs all day. There was even an outside chance that lifting and brushing them would tighten up those flappy wings that were beginning to swing from my upper arms. And tucked in the back of my mind lurked the possibility that my plump, matronly body might morph back into its long-gone seventeen-year-old figure. OK, I said it was an outside chance.

Little did I know that following in my daughter's footsteps and embarking on my new career would be like Alice in Wonderland plunging "down the rabbit hole" and into the wild and new-fangled world of mobile pet grooming. Sure, caring for pets was as old as Eve, after her fall in the Garden of Eden, pulling the burrs out of a lamb's coat. But in the 1980s my career on wheels was so innovative that, when I mentioned it, most people said, "What?"

Along the way I was privileged to meet some unique dogs, wonderfully talented groomers and generous owners. But, I also had my share of schizophrenic pets, eccentric clients and incompetent groomers, not to mention trying to herd a fleet of undependable vans.

At times, I felt I was a character in a Stephen King horror novel or involved in a newspaper account on alcoholics and druggies. I could have written Willie Nelson's *On the Road Again* or taught a course called "100 Ways to Restore Your Vehicle with Duct Tape." But my story is an actual "true confessions" yarn that includes incriminating episodes unrevealed until now. In the end I wouldn't have given up a moment (oops, well, maybe a few) of the twenty-one years I spent "Going to the Dogs."

1
You're Going to Do *What*?
· ·

When I suggested to my spouse Niel that I might be changing careers (again), he dropped the remains of his half-eaten corned beef sandwich. Choking on the bite still in his mouth, he said, "You're going to do *what*, Jan?"

I fluttered my lashes, turned up the corners of my mouth and said, "Dog grooming school! I'm going to pull my savings out of the Civil Service Retirement program and enroll in dog grooming school, just like Kris."

After doubling up with laughter, he noticed I wasn't joining in his amusement. He scratched his chin, and in a resigned whisper said, "Yeah, go ahead. I think you can do it. You've done everything else."

Was that a vote of confidence or something else? Was my long-suffering spouse referring to my seven year itch when I hop-scotched from one career to another? Perhaps my loss of hair from the stress of my current job spurred his approval, or it just may have been the willy-nilly decisions we habitually leaped into (there were those five children, you know, and we weren't even Catholic—just careless Lutherans).

Lifelong friend Lois, who could finish off a pound of Godiva chocolates and never gain an ounce, reacted in the same manner. "You're switching jobs again and going to do *what*?" followed by, "What the heck is a mobile pet groomer?"

"You know, I drive around town going from dog to dog in one of those converted vans with bathtubs and hair dryers, just like a little grooming salon."

Between bites of candy, Lois said, "Oh?" and changed the subject.

Serious-minded Son Number One, Mark, phoned from college and, making an obvious effort to joke, said, "Say, Mom, does that really pay well?"

Hearing the underlying panic in his voice that his last semester's tuition might be in jeopardy, I was about to console him when he added, "Won't that be kind of heavy work for someone your age?"

No longer concerned with soothing his fears, I retorted, "Excuse me! I'm only forty-five, Son. My muscles haven't atrophied quite yet. Besides, if I kept my nice secure government job, you might be putting me in a mental hospital, and who would pay your college costs then? Huh, huh?"

My seventy-year-old mom, always cautious, was the last to shoot an arrow into my high spirits. She frowned and said, "You spent eighteen years in college while raising five children and you're throwing all that education away on *what?*"

I attempted to have a conversation with God about whether dog grooming was really in the picture, but He wasn't plugging in. Possibly, even He was stunned by my dubious future career path and struck voiceless. But I felt I needed to rush this decision-making process along before I was reduced to purchasing a wig.

In retrospect, I should have asked myself those questions my inter-generational support groups were asking, but I chose to dismiss their concerns. Plus, in my haste to scramble into another career, I overlooked a second clue to which I ought to have paid more attention.

When Kris graduated she worked for the *only* mobile pet grooming company in the area. Why only one? Similar to *thriving* furniture stores locating their businesses within walking distance of each other, Baltimore should have had more than one mobile pet grooming firm.

Instead, we preferred to view minimal competition as an *asset,* an unfulfilled opportunity we had cleverly unearthed, and an argument for why we should go into this business. Several years later we realized this hint should have been filed in the *debit* column. But at that point I watched with envy as perky Kris trotted off each morning, swinging her little grooming kit, to play with doggies (or so I thought). Meanwhile, I trudged to my tension-filled job, where I could no longer distinguish black from white and my problem solving plummeted into shades of gray.

I enlisted my wisdom genes about whether to take the final plunge. I was totally ignorant of how to start and operate a corporation, or (and I was to find this extremely important) how to keep one solvent. My former jobs were ones where I followed someone else's orders. If I changed gears, I'd be hanging out there with no previous experience.

Niel and I knew nothing about operating a business. Although his parents owned a Dairy Queen, no business savvy had rubbed off on him. My only venture into personal sales was selling Christmas cards before I was old enough to get my work permit.

After I had dropped my bombshell about quitting my job to become a pet groomer, but before I had done the deed, Niel said, "Maybe you should get some advice on this and see what you're getting into."

I felt he wasn't quite as thrilled about my new career choice as I was, and perhaps he hoped a dose of reality would change my mind. But, ever the supportive spouse (and probably to keep an eye on his impulsive wife), he enrolled with me in the Small Business Administration's seminar for new owners.

After attending evening classes for three weeks, an attorney was assigned to give us the benefit of his experience. Why an attorney? Simple, the Baltimore area with its one and only mobile pet grooming business had no retired owners. Since our concerns seemed to be of a legal nature, we were given Mr. Sandler.

From his neck up he appeared to be an aging hippie with the prerequisite ponytail, and '60s granny glasses. From the neck down was an attempt at high fashion with his striped Versace suit—but then I spotted Indian moccasins on his feet. Mr. Sandler flipped through our master business plan. He asked a few questions, sighed and touched his lips with his index finger. "My job here is to discourage you from opening a business."

Excuse me! Instead of helping, this guy was discouraging us? I clutched Niel's hand and nearly stopped breathing, as Mr. Sandler launched into a fifteen minute discourse on new businesses statistics. The figures for failure were daunting. Did anyone last more than five years?

I didn't know about Niel, but I was ready to grab my coat, leave, and forget about my goofy idea, when Mr. Sandler finished with, "…but you folks have constructed a good business plan. I believe you're going to make it, so I'll help you navigate."

I exhaled. All right! How good was that? My professional advisor was giving me the go-ahead, even though his comments were littered with caution. Much later I would recall that Mr. Sandler knew nothing about mobile grooming, and it would have been a big help if the SBA had assigned us an expert in truck repair.

Suddenly, any last minute doubts about my decision were purged. I resigned from my $30,000 a year job, signed the "Discharge from Federal Employment" paperwork and walked out—a free woman. I shelled out $2,000 (in 1984 dollars) and confidently enrolled in pet grooming school.

On the first day of class, five other giggly students, all younger than four of my five children, followed me into the school's back room. Besides our age difference, it was also obvious that I was carrying the leftover poundage from my kiddies' births. We didn't have much in common, and I felt like Mother Goose leading a gaggle of goslings.

I was taken aback, again, when our five-foot-tall, wiry instructor, Tanya, ambled in. Sporting hip-hugging jeans, topped by a faded, tattered smock spotted with blood, and her feet encased in steel-toed shoes, she wasn't the professional I had anticipated. But what really bowled me over was her shaved head.

As she pointed to a large poster illustrating more than one hundred dogs, my attention kept wandering to that bloody smock and her bald head. I hoped the blood was hers, rather than a dog's, although that brought up even more disturbing images. I wondered if her lack of hair was due to stress and she'd lost it for the reason I had been losing mine. Either way, Tanya was one tough-looking lady.

She addressed us in her gravelly, no-nonsense smoker's voice. "You will be expected to memorize all groups of dogs and identify each breed within its group." While pointedly searching each of our faces, Sergeant Tanya added, in case we thought she was kidding, "And there will be a final exam."

Unaware that dogs were divided into groups, I glanced at my fellow students, but they didn't seem as awed by her remarks as I was. I guessed they were much more into dogs, or since most were fresh out of high school, had lost all respect for authority.

I searched the chart for a familiar breed and spotted a cocker spaniel. Yippee, I knew that one! But next to it was an identical dog called an English cocker spaniel, and next to that another one labeled a springer spaniel. Darned if I could tell them apart. And see there, an Afghan. Uh, no, the caption said "saluki." I'd never heard of that one—it looked just like an Afghan. In fact, the longer I studied the pictures, the more several breeds appeared the same. What had I gotten myself into?

I took my chart home, clipped out each dog and pasted it onto a small flash card. (I remembered Dick and Jane from first grade, but I should have paid more attention to Spot.) I enlisted the remaining child at home, thirteen-year-old David, to flash them at me.

Ever the smart aleck, he smirked and said, "Didn't we do this when I was in kindergarten, Mom?"

"Very funny. It's called payback."

I coughed up $150 for a fake-alligator-skin-covered grooming kit holding an assortment of one electric clipper, five blades, a nail clipper, scissor, brush, comb and a wicked looking hair de-matting device. While admiring this remarkable single-bladed piece of equipment, I discovered it could be lethal when I gashed my finger.

That evening Niel, noting my bandaged hand, asked, "Dog bite?"

"No, tool bite!" I barked.

During Week One, Tanya taught us groomer-wannabes dog physiology and how muscles, bones and tendons interacted. Bored, I tried not to nod off. But our instructor caught my attention the day she demonstrated how to sculpt hair to disguise faults in a breed. At one disconcerting session, she scissored the hair on a dog's head to camouflage an empty eye socket. Yep, I was wide awake for that one.

The students in the class preceding ours by six weeks clipped, seemingly with ease, hair on teensy weensy toy poodle feet. Amazed, I watched them shape poodle topknots and schnauzer beards. I winced when they plucked out ear hair with forceps. Ouch!

I grumbled to Niel, "I'm not sure I'll ever be able to do that." But I had already burned my bridges.

Week Two found me cleaning cages, and bathing and brushing out dogs. Oh, yes, I also put into action my one transferable skill gleaned from years of cutting hair for the six other family members. I was my class's top dog in hair sweeping.

"I could have done this at home," I complained to Niel. "I'm paying them $2,000 for this? They should pay me!"

He ignored my comments. No sympathy there. He was probably taking side bets from friends on how long I'd last.

That same week, like a soldier with his rifle, I learned how to take apart, clean and reassemble my clippers. My equipment and I, however, saw no action. I had yet to get my hands on the enemy—oops, I mean "practice dog." In anticipation, I'd already named it Foo-Foo, but wondered, "Where was it?"

Hallelujah! In Week Three I was finally introduced to my very own practice dog. However, Foo-Foo wasn't moving because Foo-Foo, in fact, was not a dog. What rested on my grooming table was a round wooden log covered in fake fur. I was to learn clipping technique on this?

Tanya grinned when she saw my disappointment and like a master sergeant bellowed, "You thought you were going to get a live dog to work with? Not on your life!"

What a bully. And how dare she question my clipping non-expertise.

After the first day, my log resembled a ribbed piece of corduroy with gouges, uneven patches and bald spots. Had it been a live animal, blood would have soaked the table.

Tanya wiggled her nose and sniffed as she strolled past my grooming table. With her chin in the air and hooded eyes, she looked down at my practice "dog" disdainfully. "Tut-tut," she said. "Not so easy, is it?"

What a hateful person!

On the other hand, she was right. Twenty-five years of cutting my family's hair didn't transfer to clipping dog fur. Still, by the end of the third week, I was zipping right along on my hair log, each time reducing the number of nicks and gouges. Maybe I could do this. My confidence inched skyward.

During Week Four, Tanya handed me my first live subject. At least, I assumed it was alive. Lying before me was a black, matted-to-the-skin lump of damp fur emitting that inner-city, alley-dog odor. Foo-Foo was a smelly, wriggling mess, with two black eyes poking out from masses of hair. Somewhere under those mats must be ears and legs, but where did they attach to a body? I had no idea where to begin.

"Be careful you don't nick that dog," Tanya warned.

Refusing to be intimidated by someone ten years my junior, I glared at her and retorted, "This dog is in terrible condition. How can you expect me to clip this?"

With typical sarcasm, she snarled, "Hon, welcome to dog grooming."

What Tanya lacked in teacher etiquette and diplomacy, she made up for in knowledge. She snatched the scissors out of my hand and cut through the hair by placing one edge of the scissor against the dog's body and snipping along until a few inches of skin showed. Demonstrating how to lay the clipper along that path, she cautiously inched it forward and the hair came off in a pelt.

I was amazed. If this career failed, I could move west and shear sheep.

Following her technique, I completely scalped Foo-Foo until he had less hair than he was born with. Still, he looked so cute with that fluffy little pom-pom on top of his head and tail.

Stepping back from the grooming table to admire him, I couldn't help but grin. I had performed this miracle. I had taken a dog in miserable shape and transformed him into a lovable, happy, grateful pet. My Foo-Foo was smiling, too. Yes, he was. He smelled so good. He pranced about, his big black eyes sparkled, and he seemed to know that, though bald, he was beautiful.

I was hooked. Grooming wasn't simply career choice number eight. Grooming was going to be my life's mission. From that moment I fell in love with my new occupation and the pets that owners were gracious enough to entrust to me.

Eventually, I became the speediest dog shaver in the class. I say "shaver" because I discovered that clipping off all the hair was the only possible style for the majority of our practice pups. Most arrived in a matted condition similar to Foo-Foo's.

We became pros at preparing owners for how their pets would look after we denuded them. When they dropped off their matted dog, we gave them a worst case scenario, hoping it would lessen the shock when they first glimpsed their naked loved ones. We practiced developing clever dialogues with each other before using them on a customer, but there really was no proven method of avoiding their round-eyed astonishment when they saw their sweet little dogs resembling rats.

Typically, the pre-clipping conversation went like this: "You want me to leave a little puff on the head? That I can do, but the rest of it—I'll try to salvage a bit of tail hair." Or I'd say, "You'd like Harry to look like this picture? Well, I can try, but since his fur is so matted, I'll have to charge an extra twenty-five dollars. You know, it's really torture for dogs when I have to comb the matted hair and pull it through the tangled live hair." The word "torture" always got to them, and they flinched while visualizing their pet in pain. After they agreed to the buzz cut, I'd say, "Well then, I must warn you Harry is not going to look anything like your picture."

After the grooming, their replies ranged from the complimentary, "He still looks darn cute," to "He smells better." A few owners attempted to make the best of it and said, "Oh, I love the scarf."

Somewhere along my educational path, I realized I wasn't going to be *playing* with dogs. For one thing, dogs in extremely matted conditions were not adorable. For another, they were more apt to bite my hand than lick it after they smelled doggie odors emanating from my table. Escape, not fun, was first and foremost on their minds.

Perhaps I missed the class on wrestling holds to get the job done, and I was woefully deficient in the assertiveness required to dominate "Alpha" dogs. I jumped whenever a dog shifted on the grooming table. If an animal insisted it was in charge, so be it. Biting dogs snapped and romped through my dreams. I vowed that nasty dogs weren't going to be scheduled in my business. My specialty would be wimps.

Nearing the end of the course, I passed the practical grooming tests on a cocker spaniel, three poodles, a Lhasa apso, and a bichon frise with flying colors. But during my schnauzer final, trouble reared its ugly head. After I finished grooming the first one, Tanya sauntered over to inspect my finished product.

She raised her eyebrows, puckered her lips, and presumably as an object lesson for the entire class to hear, announced, "I can see you really have no idea what the standard is for this breed!"

Surprised she would confront her oldest student ever, I stuttered, "Who, me?"

She scooped up the dog, placed him on her table and demonstrated how to correct my faulty grooming. Humiliated that I had failed my last practical test, I felt angry and defenseless as Tanya pointed out each grooming error. The other students eyed me with sympathy—though happy not to be the one picked on.

Several weeks later, I had a chance to redeem myself when a client brought in another schnauzer. Meanwhile, I had observed my fellow students working with them and hoped I had picked up enough technique to pass this time. I was almost finished and the dog looked sharp, when, oops, I nicked his ear. Blood everywhere! Instant failure! Bad dreams! I had visions of becoming a permanent student stuck in grooming school purgatory. My hard-won confidence plummeted.

Our class was in its final week. Each morning, when owners brought in their pets, I peeked around the corner from my grooming station, hoping a schnauzer would be dropped off. Hooray. On the last day one was brought in, and I snatched it from its owner's arms. This time I scissored the correct pattern, and my clipping was smooth and nick-free.

Searching for mistakes, Tanya examined my schnauzer, and I could hear the reluctance in her voice when she said, "Well, I guess you made it after all." That was the most encouraging thing she said to me during the twelve-week course.

I didn't care. Goodbye limbo. Hello graduation. Party time!

2
Going Mobile

Halfway through my grooming school education, Niel and I had a discussion about how to get my new business off the ground. The first item on the agenda was to thrash out opening a brick-and-mortar salon versus going mobile.

This was a wee bit of a problem. Other than my six weeks in grooming school and Kris' experiences, our combined knowledge of either was limited. Since mobile grooming was a new enterprise, little information existed about expenses or possible income. We couldn't pick the competition's brains either. I imagined they'd be thrilled that we were entering their formerly cornered market.

However, we had never let the lack of information deter us from making a decision before. So why now? Niel and I, using Kris' actual experiences, brainstormed every advantage and disadvantage for both options. We drew a line down a sheet of paper and wrote down every plus or minus we could come up with for each option (Kris had the most to offer about the actual mobile part).

After tallying up and batting a lot of other nuts-and-bolts considerations back and forth, it became obvious that we were leaning more toward a van operation. So we decided to go with a state-of-the-art, cutting-edge, on-the-road unit, and not open a stodgy run-of-the-mill grooming salon.

Decision made, it was time to purchase a van. Niel helped me research ready-to-go vans. He found a few firms that designed and custom built new units, but they were too costly for our seat-of-the-pants company. Pre-owned, already outfitted grooming vans didn't exist in this fledgling industry in the 1980's, so we opted for a used version. Since we had years of experience camping with recreational vehicles and were familiar with water pumps, holding tanks, electrical wiring and power converters, we felt confident we could design our own van.

We turned to Mike's Auto Repair, our dependable car repair shop, for van advice. Mike crawled out from underneath a beat-up truck and turned off a hissing cutting torch. He laid down a severed tailpipe and wiped his oily hands on a greasy rag.

"Hi, Jan and Niel, what brings you down here?"

"Say, Mike," I said, "you know we're trying to get this mobile pet grooming business off the ground. Which make of van would be the best choice for us?"

He jerked his thumb toward the rusty one he was working on. "Well, if you're going to get a used one, that make holds up pretty well. There's lots of them out there, and you should be able to find one in fairly good condition. When you do, bring her down and I'll run it through inspection. Lots more parts available for them, too."

I said, "Thanks for your opinion, Mike. We'll keep that in mind." I hoped to find one similar to the one he was working on, minus the rust.

The van had so turned me off, that I missed the operative word in his advice: "parts." We were unaware that, no matter which van we bought, we would become familiar with, and ever more dependent on, junkyards—also known as salvage businesses. The hunt to locate an elusive discontinued part would take us as far as Indian reservations in New Mexico. But for the moment, we were happy to act on Mike's recommendation. After all, he, like Mr. Sandler, was the "professional."

I didn't anticipate that every week, at least one of our vans would occupy a spot in Mike's shop. Almost single-handedly, we funded his early retirement. What were we thinking, checking with the person who had a vested interest in repairing our van?

Having decided to "go mobile," I now had to figure out the van layout and equipment.

While I learned basic grooming, Kris kept working at the other mobile company, and I assigned her the role of "spy."

"Mom, here's what it looks like," she explained, drawing a big rectangle and labeling little boxes inside it. "You have to get someone to put a high-top roof on it first. The tub is across the rear with the water systems and holding tanks underneath. She continued drawing until only a tiny place remained inside the boxes.

Alarmed that I hadn't considered whether I, too, would fit in the van, I asked, "Say, Kris, exactly how big is that little spot in the middle?"

Knowing exactly what I was getting at, she said, "Oh, Mom, I think you'll fit. It's sort of like working in a compact, cozy kitchen."

Now that I had an idea of what should be inside the van, it was time to track down someone who would work with me in creating my perfect mini-salon design.

Enter Lenny.

I discovered Lenny's Van Conversion in a small strip mall as I was tooling along Route 40. A nifty high-top van with great detailing sat in front of an unimposing store. I slammed on the brakes, U-turned and parked in front. No one was behind the service counter when I entered, but I heard the door buzzer alert.

"Anyone here?" I shouted.

"Coming," bellowed a deep voice from the rear of the store. Within a few seconds a scruffy, six-foot-tall, overweight guy dressed in a too-small-for-him plaid hunting shirt, torn camouflage cut-offs and flip-flops strolled into the waiting room.

As I described my ideas, Lenny's eyes grew big and his mouth twitched into a lopsided grin. I could tell he was visualizing the actual construction and was chomping at the bit to extend his van conversion expertise to a new project.

He confirmed his boredom with his everyday van alterations when he hitched up his pants and confessed, "I'm getting downright sick with this run-of-the-mill van stuff. Do ya know how many high-powered stereo systems I put in? And let me tell ya about the fur lined interiors." Lenny winked at me before he continued, "Betting ya know about those spur-of-the-moment romantic passion beds I put in after we rip out the seats. Ya got the right person here with me. I can do a bang-up job on whatcha want."

I considered walking out, but his fantastically converted model van out front, plus Lenny's tacky linoleum, kept my feet glued to the floor. Keeping an arm's length from Lenny, who was leaning over the counter into my personal space, I showed him the diagram I created. We discussed the arrangement of water tanks and electrical lines, and he nodded his head. At the time, I presumed his nodding signified he agreed with my suggestions. Down the line, when the actual construction began and our conversation seemed to have been forgotten, I wondered whether his bobbing head was just one of many tics.

After we agreed on a price, he hitched up his pants again, squinted and said, "You gotta van yet? Cause if ya don't, I gotta cousin who's gotta cargo van for sale. Think it's in pretty good shape. Wanna take a look-see?"

With the benefit of hindsight, I now know to be wary of people who recommend a relative's business. But based on Lenny's "professional" experience, I bribed Niel, with a promise of pizza, to accompany me to the cousin's used car lot.

The proposed van didn't look too bad. Taking Mike up on his offer to check for major defects, we drove it to his repair shop. Other than commenting, "Well, it's got a lot of miles on it, but looks pretty good," he gave it a thumbs up. We bought it.

Maaco car painters sprayed it a 1976 Corvette Blue, and how that metallic finish sparkled! We never considered that between Baltimore's blistering summer sun and the nicks, scratches and emerging rust patches we had to paint over, it would eventually turn into a blue-spotted leopard. There was a reason why most service vehicles were white—but what the heck, right then my blue baby was gorgeous!

Lenny immediately began constructing its innards. However, I soon learned to keep an eye on him. In theory, he was supposed to follow my design; in practice, he ignored it. One afternoon when I stopped in for a progress check, I was dismayed to discover Lenny had installed a hip-high grooming table. He had paid no attention to my suggestions.

"Lenny, that table has to be adjusted to waist height. I'll have chronic back pain leaning over a table that low."

Huffing and puffing out his cheeks, Lenny insisted he didn't recall our previous discussions and said, "Well, I guess I could raise it, but it looks better to me this way."

"Lenny, that's beside the point. I can't groom dogs if the table is half-way to the floor."

Lenny shrugged, "Don't blame me when ya get a big-un on that table and his head's hitting the ceiling."

"Just do it, Lenny!"

It was around Week Nine at Tanya's school, and before Lenny finished my van, that my friend Ginny found out about my new profession. "Jan, I heard you are almost through your dog grooming class. Would you be interested in practicing on my Irish setter and giving him a bath?"

I made an attempt to decline. "Ginny, I don't have my van ready to go yet."

"Oh, I figured that. You can groom him in my bathtub. I'll supply the towels and hair dryer."

I pondered her offer. I was aware that no money would exchange hands, but I needed the practice on a breed I hadn't worked with yet. "OK, I'll do it," I said.

Later that week after a long school day, I packed up my grooming tools and traveled to Ginny's suburban McMansion home. As her doorbell rang out the well-known hunt theme from Rossini's "William Tell Overture," I peeked through the door's stained glass windows and made out a galloping streak of red charging my way. The huge Irish setter threw himself at the door while barking as though I were the dreaded postman. Saliva was dripping down his neck.

Ginny yelled, "Reds, down! I said, Down!" as she attempted to collar him. "Come in, Jan, he's OK once he gets to know you." Yeah, right!

As I squeezed between the door and Reds, I tried to recall what I had learned about Irish setters...friendly, yep; perpetual teenagers, yep; hard to control, uh-oh.

Reds jumped all over me as I tugged him toward the bathroom. I shut the door, told him to "sit" (which he didn't), and attempted to grab him while he circled me. I was the Westward Ho wagon surrounded by Indians. When catching him and tying his leash to something solid failed, I decided to forgo brushing and just bathe him.

Reds obeyed me when I asked him to jump into the tub—and just as quickly jumped out. He hesitated, then hopped in again—and out. Oh, what fun he was having! I was not.

"Reds, stay," I commanded. The next time he bounded into the tub and before his long legs propelled him out again, I knotted his leash around the faucet. "Aha, gotcha now!"

Speedy Gonzales-style, I turned on the shower, soaped Reds up and rinsed him off. He loved his shampoo and bath, and I thought I was home free. I stretched behind me to grab a towel, and Red decided this was a good time to shake.

Helpless, I knelt and closed my eyes as water flew off him and onto the expensive Italian tile floor, the elegant sink and unelegant me. In fact, the entire bathroom looked like a river had flooded its banks and left red debris. Even the globe on the ceiling had strings of red hair hanging from it.

Reds slurped a sloppy kiss on me as I hauled him from the tub. He was one happy dog living up to his breed's reputation. I considered drying him and reconsidered in the same instant, as I visualized additional fur loosening up and adding another red layer.

"Ginny!" I screamed and heard frantic footsteps heading our way.

She opened the door, realized what had happened to her previously tidy bathroom, shot a look that could kill at me, and dragged an ecstatic, dripping Reds out.

Not regretting that I hadn't clipped Reds, I packed my damp tools into their equally damp box. An hour later I had finished gathering Reds' hair and used more than a dozen towels to sop up every exposed surface. Me? I was totally soaked.

Was I making a huge mistake in thinking I could groom animals that had no intention of cooperating? I was depressed and ready to give up right then and there, until I remembered I'd be doing this in my nifty van with the proper restraining devices and equipment. I vowed that in the future I would not groom a pet in its own home. What's odd is that during the next twenty-one years, no one ever asked me to. Nor was I ever asked to groom another exuberant Irish setter.

Funny, my friendship with Ginny survived in spite of what happened. But, although she went through several dogs over the years, she never again called on my services.

Lenny was almost finished with converting my van. Although certain design and construction hiccups we never really resolved would become obvious down the line, for now, excitement built as my mobile pet salon rolled out of Lenny's shop and into our driveway. It sat there, a thing of beauty. Niel and I basked in our accomplishment (did you notice he was beginning to get on board with my project?). With just a hint of smugness that I was years ahead in my unique business, I was sure success was just around the corner.

I had mulled over some names for my new business. I remembered Mr. Sandler, our attorney, warning about using a name that would limit expansion such as "Best Little Grooming Van." Only one? Also, I knew a name identifying the owner wasn't a smart idea. "Jan's Grooming Parlor" wouldn't attract a future buyer, unless her name was Jan. So I decided on the "sez-it-all" name of "Canine Clippers Mobile Pet Groomers."

While gazing and marveling at my van, I realized I needed to paint not only my company name and all-important phone number on it, but also a logo. Our son Mark had just graduated with a bachelor's degree in industrial design. He was camping out in his old bedroom in our basement while filling out job applications, and I figured the moment had arrived for him to return our five-year investment.

"Mark," I said, "how would you feel about creating a logo for our business? I'm thinking about a small dog begging to be groomed."

"Sure, Mom. It'll give me some experience and I can include it in my portfolio."

Within an hour Mark whipped up a cartoon pup standing on its hind legs and holding a pair of scissors in its mouth. That adorable doggie was just begging its owner to phone Canine Clippers for a grooming. It was perfect. I transferred the design onto business cards, stationery, receipts and my roving grooming parlor.

As Mark, Niel and I were admiring the result in our driveway, our neighbors sauntered over. After making some small talk and approving our efforts, they scrutinized the logo again and asked, "Does that dog have scissors stuck through its neck?"

I spun around. Sure enough, what I perceived as a cute little dog with its paws in the air holding scissors in its mouth could just as well be interpreted as a case of animal cruelty. This was no way to advertise a loving pet grooming service.

I reflected that perhaps hiring a family member straight out of college wasn't my best move. But it was too late to change the image on my rolling billboard and my printed material. It was our logo for twenty-one years, and I found myself repeatedly reassuring clients we were not about to sever their beloved pets' heads from their bodies.

Son Number Two, Scott, newly returned from the U.S. Air Force, was also living back home. I asked him, 'How would you feel about taking over office duties until you find a job?"

"Sure, Mom, no problem," he said, and he was good—even excellent—at it, as he juggled phone calls and a beer. In fact, my extroverted son was so over-the-top chatty, he picked up a date or two during extended "business" conversations.

Although Niel wisely kept his day job as a senior budget analyst with the Social Security Administration, he helped me set up an accounting system and created a computer file for tracking customers and their pets. He seemed to be unaware of his increasing partnership in my business.

Son Number Three, Jeff, immersed himself in out-of-state college studies and made an appearance every other month or so to monopolize the family washer and dryer and hang out with his buds. He basically disappeared.

I tried to recruit our youngest, David, to pitch in with housecleaning, but suddenly he was loaded down with homework. "Mom, Mrs. Crosby assigned science projects, and I've really got to do some research." He haunted the library during the next several weeks.

Meanwhile, Kris and I molded ourselves into a mother/daughter pet grooming dream team, sharing both office and grooming duties.

Was this family business primed to take off? You betcha!

There was, however, one teensy problem. We were ready to go, but had no place to go to.

Ever creative in getting myself out of jams, I came up with a couple of marketing strategies. Choice Number One was to place a coupon in one of those monthly mailers. But the next one being printed targeted areas located twenty miles from "Base" (the upscale name for our driveway). Considering fuel expenses, I wasn't thrilled to run a van halfway across the city.

Choice Number Two involved tucking advertising circulars under windshield wipers on vehicles parked in lots closer to base. There was a remarkable absence of family enthusiasm for that choice. I chose the first option along with placing ads in a few neighborhood newspapers.

Gradually, the office phone began to ring and appointments were scheduled. Kris and I, along with my sparkling van, toured Baltimore's roads grooming dirty dogs and cats. Since the two of us plus one animal were too many in our limited space, we took turns running the van. The groomer who stayed home helped Scott man the phones. It worked out very well. Or at least I thought so.

About five weeks into our team effort, Kris announced, "You know, this is really hard, dirty work. And it's so hot in this van."

Dumbfounded that she hadn't picked up this occupational flaw from her first grooming job, much less mentioned it to me, I spit dog hair from my mouth and said, "It sure is. What's your point?"

Her point was that she returned to college. I wasn't totally surprised, but I wished those "stick-to-the-job" family genes, rather than my "jumping-jack" ones, had risen to the surface. Then my dispatcher/ secretary son found a *real* job rather than working for his mom, and I was left to fly solo.

Although disappointed that my kids deserted me, I wasn't discouraged. I was positive my career would eventually propel me to be featured as the top groomer in *Baltimore Magazine's* annual "Best Of" issue.

I shouted to no one in particular, "Look out, Baltimore, here I come!

3
Wha-ja-say?

With both Kris and Scott opting out of my business, I thought I could handle the phone, answering machine and grooming alone. I enjoyed hopping into my van three days a week and equally loved my Mondays, Wednesdays and Fridays when I slept in until the first call woke me.

Within a month the business grew faster than I had anticipated and I added Wednesdays to my grooming schedule and the following month, Fridays. Canine Clippers was taking off like a greyhound.

All in all, I was delighted with how I was managing the operation, and I especially admired my own proficiency in handling phone calls. After providing a caller with the many reasons why he should use my services and having him schedule an appointment, oh, my, did I feel I was the cat's meow! Was I a smooth talker, or what?

On the other hand, I wasn't prepared for those times when I found myself taking part in bizarre phone conversations.

"Good morning! Canine Clippers. How may I help you?"

"I need to make an appointment to have my RV tuned up."

"Uh, ma'am, you've reached Canine Clippers. We are mobile pet groomers. I believe you want Freddy's Campers. Their phone number is one digit off from ours."

Aware that fifty percent of Americans owned pets, I enthusiastically added, "But if you own a dog and your pup is in need of some grooming, we're offering a five dollar discount right now. What's even better, you don't even need to leave your home. We come to you." And as brazen as that sounded, every so often I snared a new customer.

Many calls were a waste of time.

"You're not here yet! I had a 10:00 appointment. It's 10:30 and I can't sit around all day waiting for 'you people.'"

I was amused at how, when a client became upset, we became "you people."

In my best honey-dipped voice I said, "Ma'am, could I have your name to locate you on the schedule?"

"This is Mrs. Horst. I called two weeks ago for this appointment."

Quickly skimming that day's calendar, I couldn't find a Mrs. Horst. I glanced at the next several days of scheduled appointments and couldn't spot her there, either. If she was in my appointment book, her name had been written with invisible ink.

"I'm very sorry, Mrs. Horst. I'm unable to find you on today's schedule. Are you sure it was Canine Clippers that you called?" I was still friendly, but the warmth in my voice dropped a degree.

"Yes, I am! My finger's right here by your number in the Yellow Pages and I even checked it in pencil. This is Finished Dog, isn't it?"

"No, ma'am. This is Canine Clippers."

There was a soft click on the other end of the line.

Confirming appointments provoked some customers.

"Hi, Mr. Hartley, this is Jan at Canine Clippers. I'm just calling to confirm your appointment for Rosco's grooming on Saturday. I should arrive—"

Mr. Hartley cut me off. "I know when my appointment is. I have it on my calendar. Why do 'you people' keep calling me? You think just because I'm eighty-five I won't remember? If you keep calling me about these appointments, I'm not going to use your services anymore."

"Sorry, sir, but not all clients are as dependable as you. I'm sorry to have inconvenienced you—"

But irritated Mr. Hartley banged down his receiver.

Two days later, when I arrived to groom Rosco, no one was home. Our dependable Mr. Hartley had forgotten his appointment.

Baltimore's population was ethnically diverse, and some calls went like this:

"Hi, Canine Clippers here, returning your phone call."

"Hola, no comprendo. No hablo Inglés," said an elderly woman.

Putting my high school Spanish to work, I said, "¿Es Señorita Carmen dónde?"

Uh-oh. Too late, I recalled the Spanish word for "there" was not "donde." Should I have said "está" instead of "es?"

No matter. Grandma said, "No comprendo Inglés."

So much for my bilingual effort. I said, "Muchas gracias, Señora. Adiós."

I phoned later that evening when I stood a better chance of reaching her English-speaking granddaughter. Even so, I kept my high school Spanish dictionary handy for future conversations.

On another call, when I asked for Jesse Brown, I heard a woman scream, "Jesse, get down here! Some white woman on the phone for you."

I waited. A quiet, seemingly embarrassed teen picked up the phone and confirmed his pet's appointment. At least we were communicating in English.

At the time, the second largest Jewish population in the U.S., after New York City, was located in Baltimore. Therefore, it was no surprise that Jews receiving permission to leave Russia immigrated to our area.

"Hi there, this is Jan from Canine Clippers. I'm trying to reach Mrs. Stafonovich."

The Russian grandma practicing her English on me was about as proficient as I was in speaking Russian. We struggled for mutual under-standing until a younger voice, speaking perfect English, took over.

Yet, despite the occasional language barrier, word traveled fast about the new groomer in town. Many evenings I came home to my office and saw the number "30" blinking on the answering machine. Yikes. Responding to those calls could ruin my evening as I gobbled snacks and returned messages. Most were routine. But frequently, there were mystery calls that challenged my deciphering skills.

A female voice announced, "I need...for...cancel...but...Friday...483."

Phooey! I searched the caller ID for a number containing "483." No luck. Were there *any* appointments for Friday that included those digits? No. Was she possibly canceling an appointment for some other day and wanted to switch to a Friday? Who *was* this person and what did she want?

If the call couldn't be tracked, chances were I would arrive at someone's home at some point only to belligerently be told, "I canceled that appointment. Don't 'you people' ever listen to your messages?"

Sometimes I recruited Niel for a second opinion as I replayed a message over and over. "Did you get that? What do you think that number was?"

Just as stumped as I was, he'd say, "Got me."

In every business, as much as one attempts to deliver a quality product, things go wrong. In those cases, the customer would call me (a.k.a. "The Complaint Department") to vent. A typical conversation went like this:

"Hi, Canine Clippers, how can I help you?"

"My dog doesn't have any hair left!"

Astonished, I responded, "What did you say?"

"You heard me. You skinned Ziggy."

Switching from secretary to detective mode, I checked the caller ID and said, "Mrs. Ashe, your dog's hair was so matted that I had to shave him. You weren't home and I couldn't contact you, but I told your housekeeper to tell you that when you returned."

"She didn't tell me anything, and I've *never* had him come in from a grooming looking like this. It will take months before he grows back any hair. You'll never touch my Ziggy again!"

Fortunately, I had saved what could best be described as a one-piece-pelt, just in case Mrs. Ashe lodged a complaint with the Better Business Bureau.

Confident and ready for battle, I said, "M'am, I could swing by tomorrow and show you the terribly matted fur I clipped off Ziggy."

But Mrs. Ashe wasn't interested in explanations, "Harrumph. I'm stopping payment on my check. And what's more, I'm telling all my friends who get their dogs groomed by you what happened. You won't get any more business from this neighborhood."

Win some, lose some; and sometimes I didn't care.

Frequently, I became wedged between family members who had opposing views as to how they wanted their pet groomed.

"This is Mrs. Radison. You were here today and I specifically left a picture of how I wanted Sammy to look. You didn't follow any of my directions. Sammy's got no hair left."

"Well, Mrs. Radison, when I arrived, Mr. Radison showed me the photo and your note saying you wanted one inch of hair left. But your husband said he wouldn't pay to have his dog groomed again in six weeks and ordered me to shave it off."

When I finally convinced her I had only followed directions from the person who handed me Sammy, she paused and said, "Oh, OK. But the next time 'you people' come, don't pay any attention to Mr. Radison. He's got nothing to say about Sammy. Sammy's *my* dog!"

Mrs. Radison fancied "cute." Mr. Radison demanded "thrift" and his money's worth. I knew I would be invariably caught in the middle and was tempted not to answer when I spotted their number on the caller ID.

Finally, there were the phone calls regarding parking issues. Baltimore's Inner Harbor residents lived in two-hundred-year-old narrow homes built in rows a block long and featuring the city's famous marble steps and unique painted screen doors. Between tourists trying to catch a glimpse of them and residents' cars taking up the few spaces available, parking was at a premium.

Kris was still working with me when a call came in from a customer living on one of those narrow streets. "Your groomer's here and she says she won't groom my dog!"

"Did she say what the problem was?"

"She says she's got nowhere to park her van."

"Well, when you made the appointment we did discuss parking and that you needed to supply a legal parking spot close enough to your home for her to use your electrical outlet."

"I had a spot for her, but some dodo pulled in there. I told your groomer to double-park. She says she won't do it! Now listen, everyone double-parks around here. The cops *never* give *nobody* a ticket for *nothing*!"

If a double negative was a positive, was a triple negative still a negative? Either way, we weren't going to chance a thirty-dollar parking ticket. "I'm sorry, but unless she has a *legal* parking spot, we aren't able to groom your dog." And the kicker, "Unfortunately, we do have to charge a ten-dollar service fee for the hour we set aside."

"Wha-ja-say? I'm not paying no service fee. I didn't get no service. And not only that, I'm reporting you to the Better Business Bureau. I'm suing 'you people' for not grooming my dog."

Although the negatives in that sentence tickled my funny bone, I didn't dwell on it. I zeroed in on the words "I'm suing." Wait a minute! Whose loss was this anyway? It was my turn to retort, "Wha-ja-say?"

In time, I developed coping mechanisms for dealing with unhappy clients. My first technique was not to interrupt the grumblers, but allow them to finish speaking. They were puzzled that I wasn't cutting them off and protesting our business's innocence for whatever awful thing we had done. Could it be I was listening? When they ran out of steam, I said, "Tsk, tsk. You may be absolutely right, but let me see what I can do about it and I'll get back to you."

"OK, thank you, Jan. I'm sorry I got so upset. I knew you'd fix it."

After hanging up, I uttered several words that shouldn't have slipped out. I stifled a few more by pounding a pencil into my desktop. By the end of the month, my desk pad looked like a woodpecker had used it for practice.

Niel commented, "Have you considered buying stock in this company?" as he replaced yet another pad. But one replacement a month was worth having my customers think I was the most genial, soft-spoken, gracious business owner on earth.

Attempting to quell additional irritation from my clients, I tried to return messages the same day, even if it was after 10:00 p.m. It impressed customers that I was working into the wee hours of the evening just for them. Besides, putting off unpleasant conversations would haunt me until I did phone them back, and then they were twice as peeved.

Sometimes I prayed before returning a message from an unhappy client. It was amazing how often a conversation with God helped to soften one with a client, but our chats were a one-sided monologue. It irked me that at this point in our relationship, when He should be aware that He'd created an *impatient* human, He tended not to answer as promptly as I wished. Nevertheless, prayer helped me focus and keep a lid on my temper.

When all else failed, I poured an up-to-the-rim glass of cream sherry, sipped and said to the unhappy caller, "What did you say? Oh, I know what you mean. I hate it when that happens."

At first I believed there were benefits to locating my office in our home. But when I found myself hopping out of bed at 6 a.m. to catch that early morning ring-ring, I had second thoughts. And when after ten hours on the road, I encountered three hours of answering machine calls and dined that evening on fish sticks, hot dogs and a frozen microwave dinner, I considered that maybe a home office wasn't so great after all.

Mr. Sandler, our Administration attorney, had advised, "The telephone will be your lifeline."

Well, sure! It didn't take a genius to figure that out. No calls coming in equaled no van moving out. What I didn't realize was that the phone line would be attached to me like an umbilical cord.

Tired of being a slave to my answering machine, I had an idea how to reverse that and make it my servant. My thoughts went to Lois, my friend who had nonchalantly said, "Oh?" when I told her about my new career. There she was, sitting around her house doing absolutely nothing, while my life had become way too hectic. I figured she could spare a few hours and help out a couple of days a week. Good friend that she was, she agreed.

Wow! Lois was great at fielding calls and all went well for a few months, but Lois left at 2:00, and as business tripled and quadrupled, the messages piled up. I was back to where I had started. As the evening hours progressed, my speech turned raspy and my well-modulated professional voice evaporated. My usual good nature departed as well.

"Mom, I gotta talk to you," David pleaded

"Have to return these calls. Wait a sec."

Niel begged, "Jan, we need to discuss this electric bill."

Tossing it back at him with one hand and dialing a customer with the other, I snarled, "Can't you see I'm on the phone? If I don't return her call, Mrs. Himmelfarb will throw a hissy fit."

One morning Niel complained, "Some strange woman crawled in bed with me around midnight."

I gave him my nastiest look.

He wasn't impressed. "Oh, that was you?"

I could take a hint. After losing my hair in my previous job, I was on the road to losing my husband in my current one. Plus, I was dying to recapture those elusive evening hours. I first tapped Lois to see if she could add a few hours (in fact, perhaps forty), but apparently she wanted her own life back and turned me down. It was time to place an ad in *The Baltimore Sun* for part-time office help.

I peeked through the window as model-thin Nancy tottered up the sidewalk on her spiked heels. She was wearing a silk suit and a perky hat crowning braided hair extensions. Yes, a hat! I was not expecting to interview a Naomi Campbell wannabe for a part-time position. Our small office held two desks—one shared by Niel and me and the other for our new employee. As long as our new secretary/dispatcher had a friendly telephone manner, she could strut in wearing pajamas and we wouldn't blink.

I didn't see a car parked in front and presumed she was either dropped off or took the bus. During the interview I asked, "Well, Nancy, how can you assure me you'll arrive on time?"

"Miz Nieman, I know the bus routes. I won't have no trouble getting here by 9:00."

Silly me, I believed her.

I took the week off to train her on scheduling dogs, fielding inquiries and confirming appointments. While she had a pleasant phone manner, she didn't catch on as fast as I had hoped. Even though Nancy had lived in Baltimore most of her life, she had difficulty with routing. I was dismayed to find myself cruising back and forth like a ping-pong ball from one end of town to the other within the same day.

Calling her attention, again, to the zip code map on the wall, I said, "Nancy, you need to book back-to-back appointments in the same or nearby zip code." It was painful to watch her scanning back and forth across the map as though she were watching a tennis match. Even with my help, it took fifteen minutes for her to schedule an appointment.

A new client consumed even more time. Then Nancy had to jot down phone numbers and addresses. In addition, she needed to discuss the dog's temperament and grooming style, and question whether the pet was up-to-date on its rabies shots. And if the customer asked a question that wasn't on her crib sheet, the next caller was certain to be irritated by the twenty-minute busy signal.

Exhausted by the effort of each conversation, Nancy dashed to the restroom to recuperate as soon as she hung up. Within a few seconds the phone rang, and if I was in the office, I picked it up.

An irate caller would blurt, "Why don't you people get another line? I spent over forty-five minutes trying to get through!"

Nancy reminded me of Lily Tomlin's operator comedy routine: "Is this the party to whom I am speaking?" Installing a second line wouldn't have helped. She would simply have placed the incoming call on "hold" until the customer hung up.

After a week of watching her destroy my business, I realized that leaving her alone would be a dreadful move. But I had no choice. The following week I had a full schedule of appointments and Nancy would have to be on her own—for what it was worth.

Canine Clipper's office hours began at 9:00, but on Monday she hadn't arrived by 9:15. I wore a track in the carpet pacing back and forth from my desk to the window. 9:30 came and went—no Nancy. I phoned her—no answer. I placed a message on our answering machine and hit the road. Nancy never arrived. Annoyed, I spent three hours returning calls that evening.

On Tuesday, Nancy sauntered in around 9:30. "Miz Nieman, I'm sorry I couldn't make it in yesterday. I had some personal problems."

"You couldn't call and let me know?"

"No, I couldn't. I was so upset when Sol left me, I wasn't thinking straight."

Wednesday at 10:00, and no longer in stylish attire, Nancy jogged up the driveway in her running shoes and sweats. Her get-up was beginning to match her performance. I asked myself the Ann Landers question, "Am I better off with or without her?" Nancy answered that herself on Thursday when she stopped coming—period.

Lois took over the office to help out for a couple of weeks and I promised myself that in the future, I'd advise applicants of a two-week trial period. If they didn't show promise, they would be dismissed. But I really never became hard-hearted enough to enforce the policy.

The next prospect, Joan, was well qualified to man my office. Her excellent resume showed a high level of office experience, and she was up to speed within a month. We were so confident of her abilities that Niel and I took a much needed three-day mini-vacation.

When we checked in at the campground, two hours away, we were told there was a message for us. I recognized the number as Lois', but was baffled as to why she'd be calling us.

"Jan, I just received a call from your new office person. She's locked herself in the office. Chessie is stalking her."

"What did you say?" I shouted into the phone.

Lois explained that Chessie, our black stray we had taken in, was lonely and had slipped into the office to be petted. Chessie generally hung out in our basement and Joan was unaware she was sharing space with a cat. Terrified, she shooed Chessie from the office, only to have him scoot back in. When she shut the office door on him, she heard Chessie meowing on the other side. Joan, unable to contact us, had called the "emergency" number I'd left—Lois'.

I said, "Lois, call her back and tell her Chessie is harmless."

By now, our new secretary was close to hysterics, and in her mind our lonely, sweet kitty's meowing was transformed into the roar of a humongous beast ten times her size.

"Can you come over here and get the cat away from the door?" she shrieked to Lois.

"No, I can't. I have my grandchildren here. I'll have Jan call a neighbor to remove Chessie from the house."

Our neighbor came over and scooped up Chessie, who rewarded her with contented purrs. Meanwhile, Joan shouted from behind her barricade, "Did you capture the cat? Is the cat gone?"

My neighbor reassured her, "Yep, she's in my arms," and laughed when she later told me, "Joan snatched her coat and shot out the door."

She never returned—but we did.

My mini-vacation ruined, I resumed the search for office help while Lois held down the fort. She was grasping that slowly, but surely, she was being sucked into a whirlpool. Again, I offered her the job, but she declined, saying she had to be free to babysit when her daughter needed her. Huh, some buddy, and couldn't she have come up with a better excuse?

The next time I phoned *The Baltimore Sun,* the classified operator said, "Ms. Nieman, I'll keep your ad on file for easy retrieval."

Beginning to appreciate how difficult it was to find an employee who showed up promptly, liked cats and didn't monopolize my business phone, I tacked the ad on my bulletin board, so that I, too, could retrieve it easily the next time, and the next, and the next...

If it sounds as though I hired nothing but incompetent office personnel, that's actually not true. Perhaps my interviewing skills improved, because eventually I found a number of excellent and compassionate office helpers. They understood they were dealing with pet owners who cherished their animals as family members. Those employees were dependable, prompt, gave us sufficient notice when they needed a day off, and weren't "sick" at least once a week.

We were blessed to have them and they know who they are.

4

Dogs Gone AWOL

. . . .

I grew up without pets, unless you counted the birds and turtles allowed in apartments. It wasn't until I had children that I owned a dog, but Gypsy didn't require much tidying up. My first hands-on experience with dogs and cats didn't come until grooming school. But my real doggie-land education began in earnest once I began Canine Clippers.

Dogs were funny, affectionate and sometimes fearful. Dogs were smart, and when a mobile pet groomer showed up, I discovered the clever ones vanished.

The first time I knocked on Mrs. Brooks' door, her frisky black and white Shih-Tzu welcomed me with yelps of joy, jumping as though she were on a pogo stick. Oh, the excitement! For a few moments, the cutie and I were the best of pals. She was unaware she was in for the same questionable treatment she received at a grooming salon.

I knelt in front of her to get acquainted and schmoozed, "This must be Sassy. Hi, sweetie, aren't you the friendly one!"

As Sassy and I mini-bonded, Mrs. Brooks folded her hands as though in prayer, smiled and stepped back to watch. Like most pet owners, she wanted Sassy's grooming to be a pleasant experience. If all went well, she expected Sassy would greet me with similar enthusiasm in the future.

Mrs. Brooks said, "Here, let me give you this picture of Sassy. This is exactly what I want her to look like. Oh, and here's a doggie treat to give her after."

I did not disclose that once Sassy was in my grooming van, she'd be more interested in escaping than munching a tasty morsel. I dropped the snack into my smock pocket for my own pet to enjoy later.

Sassy and I strolled down her front walk, equally delighted. Her high-spirited prancing and tail wagging showed me she was thrilled to be out for a neighborhood stroll. I was relieved a tussle hadn't occurred and she willingly went with me. After all, it was bad form to drag a pet by its leash while it braced all fours against any forward movement. Owners, watching from their windows, usually frowned and wrung their hands if they spotted a groomer yanking their pup to the van.

Sassy was not one that needed encouragement. She jumped into the van and I knew she was hoping, "We're going for a ride. Oh, goody!"

The minute I placed Sassy on the table, her ears slowly drooped and her tail stopped wagging. With her superior sense of smell, I presumed she recognized doggie odors similar to those at the hated grooming salon. She had been tricked.

Sassy endured the hour of brushing, clipping, bathing and drying. Similar to my relationship with my dentist, she might personally like me, but would rather be somewhere else. She was not a difficult dog, just reluctant. She'd been through this routine before and was stoic and cooperative—a groomer's dream. I spritzed her with cologne, attached pink ribbons to her ears and sauntered to the house with her in my arms.

"Oh, doesn't she look cute," gushed Mrs. Brooks. "I'd like to make another appointment while you're here."

Six weeks later when I returned, Sassy, furiously wagging her tail like a butterfly's wings, cavorted behind her owner.

"Sassy! How are you?" I stooped to her level again. "Sassy? Are you ready for your beauty treatment?"

She swiftly reversed her forward motion, scampered away and wedged herself under the couch. Guess not.

Mrs. Brooks was appalled. "I don't know what's the matter with her. She's usually so friendly." Mulling over this turn of events, she narrowed her eyes and said, "Did something happen in the van last time?"

"No, nothing at all," I assured her, "but dogs generally don't like to be groomed. She probably remembers who I am."

Mrs. Brooks coaxed her from beneath the sofa with a doggie treat of Pup-Peroni and handed her to me. I cuddled the crestfallen Sassy as I traipsed to the van. Returning home after her second grooming, Sassy was again the frisky pup Mrs. Brooks expected. I knew better. Sassy's high spirits simply reflected her delight at escaping from that detested van. Unaware of the real reason her pup was unable to contain her joy, Mrs. Brooks was all smiles as she gave me a generous tip and scheduled another appointment.

Visit number three found Sassy again waiting at the door. This time, as soon as she spotted me, she disappeared into the bowels of her home.

"I don't think she likes you," her dismayed owner said. "She doesn't act like this with anyone else."

Using my most professional voice I assured her that Sassy's behavior was normal. "If Sassy were in a cage waiting her turn at a grooming salon, she'd be even more unhappy."

Mrs. Brooks frowned. I figured she was pondering whether to pay a service charge or allow me to groom her dog one last time. In any event, she began searching for Sassy while I folded my arms and waited at the door.

Unsuccessful at finding her, she shouted to me, "She doesn't appear to be on the first floor."

While she climbed the stairs toward the bedrooms, I checked my watch. Ten minutes had passed and Sassy was still AWOL. Thumping noises traveled down from the second floor, but no Sassy.

"She's under a bed," Mrs. Brooks called from upstairs. "She won't come out. I pushed a broom at her, but she just crawls to the other side."

"Try to get her out with a treat," I shouted up the stairwell. But I was almost positive Sassy was aware of me, and so long as I was still there, she was not to be hoodwinked by a mere puppy delicacy.

Mrs. Brooks gave up, "I just can't get her. I'm afraid we'll have to reschedule."

I was in a snit. Twenty minutes had passed and it was too late to replace this appointment with another.

I fumed and was ready to stomp out when I heard a child say, "Mommy, Sassy's afraid of Henry. Why don't you take him out of his cage and put him under the bed?"

I wondered, Who's Henry? Is he a cat? Or, worse, could he be a snake?

Mrs. Brooks later shared the scenario with me. "I told Melanie to kneel at one side of the bed with her hamster," (thank you, Lord— no snake) "and I crouched on the other. I held a leash while Melanie released Henry. The hamster edged toward Sassy, and she shot out my side of the bed." With a hint of pride and a giggle, Mrs. Brooks told me, "I sort of lassoed her."

After the roundup, I was certain Sassy would not walk to the van. I scooped her up and carried her. Breaking all grooming speed records, I did a surface job and rushed her back to her home. I half hoped Mrs. Brooks had given up on using our services, but no, she had calmed down and was searching her calendar for a future date.

"How about six weeks for Sassy's next appointment?" she suggested. "What I think you should do is phone five minutes before you arrive. That will give me time to get a leash on her."

I agreed. "That's a great idea." After all, Sassy wasn't a dumb dog, and she had concluded the van and I were a matched set; when one arrived, so did the other. This little scheme just might outsmart her.

Visits number four and five ran smoothly. I called five minutes ahead, and when I arrived, Sassy was on a leash. The humans were pleased; the canine wasn't.

I followed the procedure for visit number six, but when I arrived, Sassy was nowhere to be seen.

Mrs. Brooks, out of breath after searching for her pup, said, "She bolted the minute you phoned. I think that little stinker put two and two together when the phone rang and I went for the leash. She figured out you were coming."

I personally thought her owner was giving Sassy way too much credit for psychic abilities and pulling a Houdini. Again, Mrs. Brooks engaged Henry to flush out Sassy. This was getting silly.

Mrs. Brooks proposed another solution, "Jan, why don't you phone me when you're an hour away. Even if Sassy suspects it's you, when you don't immediately arrive, she'll forget the phone call and reappear. How about we give that a try?"

I wasn't going to hold my breath. Just how intelligent was this dog anyway? To my amazement, the ruse worked. The two of us congratulated ourselves on being one step ahead of Sassy, and from then on, I groomed Sassy without the drama.

Frequently, when clients and I had a previous relationship, they hid a key, left a check on the table, and trusted me to groom their dog in their absence. That was the situation with Prince, a delightful golden retriever who was usually happy to see me. But Prince was not the brightest pup in the litter, and not until he found himself in the van did he remember, "Oh, shucks, this is the groomer again...shouldn't have been so welcoming." Nevertheless, he was a perfect gentleman and patiently put up with his grooming. Unlike Sassy, he never connected the van with me, and each time, he appeared ecstatic when I drove up.

His bathing finished, I was ready to return Prince to his home, grab the check and travel to my next victim. I looped the leash around his neck and bent to open the sliding van door. Just as I cracked it a few inches, he pushed it wider and wedged his body through. As he shot out with his leash flying behind him, he dashed across the lawn. I, his out-of-shape groomer gasping for air, tried to keep him in sight. I did my best, but he bounded across the neighbor's front yard, whipped around the corner of the house, and vanished.

I was terrified he would gallop onto a nearby highway and get hit by a car. Out of breath and with a catch in my side, I gave up the chase. "Prince! Prince!" I shouted.

A door opened and a woman poked her head out. "Something wrong, miss?"

Oh, Lordy. I groomed another dog on this street and didn't relish rumors of today's escapade traveling through the neighborhood. I waved to her and smiled. "Nope, just Prince and me enjoying a run."

Oh, I was enjoying it all right. Drat! Where had that dog gone?

I retraced my steps while mentally composing a note of apology and explanation. As I approached the van, Prince cut around the corner, bounded up his steps, and looking entirely pleased, plunked his rear end on the porch. His tongue was hanging out one side of his mouth, and he was clearly thrilled with his morning sprint.

I knew what he was thinking. "What took you so long? Wasn't that fun? Like to do it again?" His romp over, he obediently allowed me to pick up his leash and lead him into his house.

Relieved, I prayed, "Thank you, Lord," and in spite of events, bent down to scratch him behind his ears. I said, "You are one sneaky dog, but I still love you," and received a tongue-slapping kiss in return.

Another dog, Chow-Chow, wasn't a chow at all, but a large Chesapeake Bay retriever who lived around the corner from Base. His owners worked, and since no one was home, Chow-Chow was a latchkey dog. He was easy to groom, yet he never entered the van without a *major* tug of war.

Since he weighed more than ninety pounds, I couldn't lift and carry him. The outcome of the dragging contest was always in doubt until either he was in the van and on the table, or I was forced to phone for reinforcements. I learned to schedule Chow-Chow for late afternoons when David was home from school and available to help lift.

One breezy day in early fall, I opened all the van windows. What a relief from the stifling hot summer, and, oh, that crisp air smelled so good! Chow-Chow had lost the battle to the van and after obligingly placing his paws on the table while I hefted his rear end, he was at last ready for grooming. I was proud of my victory. But as I reached for my brush, Chow-Chow leaped from the table and scrambled over the driver's seat. The open window next to him was too much of an enticement. He thrust out his head, looked both ways, and though his body was larger than the opening, worked at squeezing it through.

I lunged over the front seat and hung onto his rear to keep him in the van, but Chow-Chow had the leverage and slipped out like a greased pig.

I was horrified. Not only could he break a leg jumping from that height, but if he escaped, I had little chance of catching him. Thankfully, he darted to his front door and parked himself on the landing. I crept toward him—afraid he might be spooked and off he'd go. Instead, he stayed put until I knelt next to him.

I lied and whispered, "What a good dog you are; such a pretty boy." If he knew I was ready to murder him, he would have galloped down the block.

Cooing to him, I placed a leash around his neck and patted him, feeling around his body for tender spots or broken ribs. He didn't seem injured. I gently dragged him (how does one "gently" drag ninety pounds?) back to the van and rolled up all the windows. Another lesson learned—no matter how beautiful the day, never again did I leave windows open while grooming.

Canine Clippers had a wide service area, stretching from Baltimore's Inner Harbor to its suburbs—I even traveled to a few remaining country farms. It didn't take long to discover those working dogs were hard to fool. They had memories like elephants and never forgot a visitor. I think they smelled the van two miles away and it was impossible for me to arrive unannounced.

One morning Mr. King called to schedule his collie's annual shave-down. When I turned into the farm driveway, Dodger, all-around cow herder, chicken chaser, and guard dog, flew alongside the van. But before I came to a halt, Dodger made a U-turn and dashed out of sight. He must have sensed I was that hated once-a-year groomer.

Embarrassed, Mr. King said, "Well, Jan, I don't rightly know what to say. He's usually right here greeting every soul who drives in, whether welcome or not." He stroked his chin. "Maybe if you stick around a bit, he might show up."

Declining his invitation, I collected a service charge (a fraction of what I would have received), and drove back down the driveway. I sensed some movement through the passenger's side window and before I reached the highway, I glimpsed Dodger slinking from the woods.

He sat on his haunches, challenging me to join in round two for his amusement. For a moment I even considered turning around, but I knew who would win this game of "Find the Vanishing Dog." As I continued rolling down the farm road, I saw Dodger (aptly named) ambling back to his home.

Darn AWOL dogs!

5

All In a Day's Work

My first summer grooming, operating the business and mastering the art of staying cool in the van (or at least not passing out) was long past. Fall slid by with no real problems. But now it was mid-December, and I had to give serious thought to how and when I should travel if it snowed.

Baltimoreans didn't cope well with winter weather. In fact, if the 11:00 evening forecaster mentioned the "possibility" of white stuff, employees were primed to call in sick the next morning. Fathers, adrenalin pulsing, rolled snowblowers out of sheds, ready to do combat, and their children geared up for a day off from school. If the snow failed to materialize, they all sulked together.

Snow in Wisconsin, where I grew up, wasn't a big deal. Baltimoreans, however, had an aversion to driving in it, so I created a snow-day plan. In the morning, if it was predicted but hadn't arrived, I would stay out until it did, and then head home. If it was already snowing, I'd cancel and reschedule my appointments. I wasn't going to chance someone plowing into my bread-and-butter van or vice versa.

One December morning, after a night of rain and temperatures hovering just below freezing, black ice glazed the roads, but snow was not predicted. I was scheduled to groom dogs all the way from Base to the other side of town and back. I decided to get an early start, knowing traffic on the beltway would be slow. After de-icing the frozen door lock, I checked for running water and switched the furnace and water heater on. All systems were go.

Niel called out as he left for work, "The roads will be slick this morning. Be careful."

I grabbed my coffee mug and zipped up my waterproof smock (which never lived up to its description). Sensing little control on the slick surface, I was careful backing up, but my van had a mind of its own. It slid down the driveway, out into the court, and didn't stop until it jumped the curb across the street and stopped short of a house. I carefully drove off my neighbor's lawn to the street.

Muttering about lousy tires without traction, I considered inching back up the driveway, but decided to just keep going downhill. I knew the sand trucks would soon be on the main roads, and by the time I was finished with my first dog, the streets would be fine.

After I bullied my way onto Baltimore Beltway's fast lane, I noticed way too many red taillights glowing up ahead. Uh-oh, an accident? I shot across three lanes and zipped off at the next exit.

Fellow travelers acknowledging my brazen move held up a finger—and not a very nice one either. Several others followed my lead, and we all skated to the ramp's bottom. Together, we crawled along at ten miles per hour, about the same speed as the beltway. After months of street combat, I knew every alternate route, but no point in transferring to them today. In this weather, I suspected all of them were jammed.

I remembered Niel's words, "If you don't make a success of this dog grooming business, you could always drive a taxi."

I arrived fifteen minutes late to Mrs. Burns and her dachshund, Buster. She gave me a lukewarm welcome. In fact, she was a tad hostile. With folded arms over her chest, she shouted from her doorway, "I've been calling your office for the last half-hour to see what's happening. I have to leave in forty-five minutes for work. I told you that when I made the appointment!"

As I untangled my electrical cord and dragged it to her home, I apologized. "I'm so sorry. I gave myself over an hour to get here, but there must have been an accident on the beltway. My secretary doesn't get into the office before nine, or I would have radioed her to phone you." Trying to smooth her ruffles, I added, "But I think we'll make it. Buster only needs a touch-up today."

"Well, now, I don't want you doing a rush job."

I assured her, "Absolutely, not!"

Buster received the fastest grooming I'd ever done, and I sprinted back to the house with seconds to spare.

Mrs. Burns was anxious to get going. Since I was blocking her driveway, I hurriedly threw the electrical cord in the van and accelerated back out. In my rush to accommodate her, I had forgotten to remove my grooming box from the table. I heard the awful sound of the heavy case that held my precious equipment, sliding, then smashing onto the floor.

I pulled to the curb and discovered the case was severely damaged, plus Kwik-Stop, a yellow styptic powder, had spilled all over my tools. I inspected the equipment inside, especially my expensive scissors, and although everything seemed OK, I would have to wait until I had power again to check the clippers.

Without a minute to spare if I wanted to keep to my schedule, and hoping the Beltway was clear, I maneuvered my van into traffic and made up a bit of time. I found my way to 1213 Hooper Street, but the street was only two blocks long and although I traveled back and forth, I couldn't spot a house with the number "1213."

I radioed the office, "Jan to Base. Lois, could you phone Mr. Warner and ask him where he's located on Hooper Street? Over."

After a few minutes, Lois radioed, "Base to Jan. Jan, he says he's on Hooper *Road*, not Hooper *Street*. Over."

Phooey. I examined Mr. Warner's file, and sure enough it read Hooper *Road*. I checked my map. "Lois, I'm not too far from him. Tell him I should be there in fifteen minutes."

"Will do. Clear." I snapped the mic back into the receiver.

But Lois was back on. "Base to Jan. I better warn you he's not a happy camper. He said, 'I hope "you people" get it right next time, if there is a next time.' Clear."

I found Hooper Road, but it was one of those dead-end alleys that the Baltimore City Department of Transportation saw fit to name. How could I park halfway down and not block the remainder of the alley? Aware I would be late for the rest of the day, I was tempted to forget about Mr. Warner. But those German responsibility genes kicked in, and grabbing my cord, I climbed the fifteen rickety steps to his apartment.

Jolted by a deep "Arf, arf," I lost my balance and almost tumbled back down. Grabbing the railing, I looked up to see an enormous hairy dog standing on its hind legs with its snoot pressed to the door's windowpane. The woofing continued until Mr. Warner shuffled to the door.

I was in a snit. Not only did I not have a safe place to park, but we had recently decided to not groom dogs weighing more than fifty pounds. Who scheduled this giant?

Ticked off, I didn't bother to introduce myself and dove right in. "Mr. Warner," I began, "Canine Clippers has a weight limit on the dogs we groom. Didn't we discuss this with you when you called?"

Mr. Warner straightened to his full height and thrust his head forward. Nose to nose, he said, "Now you just hold on, Missy. Pal here ain't the dog getting groomed." He picked up a tiny Chihuahua. "This here's Pedro. He's the one getting cleaned up…and you're mighty late, and arriving with a bad attitude, yet."

Chastised again, I retreated. "Oh, I'm sorry." This seemed to be my day for perpetual apologies.

I checked Pedro's rabies certificate, and with the tiny Chihuahua in my arms, I carefully managed the wobbly stairs. I was almost back to the van when a car pulled up behind me.

"Lady," the driver yelled, "you're blocking the alley!"

I shouted back, "Yes, I know, but there's nowhere else to park!"

Climbing into my van and slamming the door, I figured he'd either park behind me, which would be problematic when I left, or he'd pound on the door until I backed out. I visualized him copying down the van's twelve-inch-high phone number and calling the cops.

I checked the rearview mirror, but, whoopee, he'd left. I presumed these alley residents encountered parking incidents on a daily basis and simply dealt with them.

Pedro was in and out of the van in half an hour. Although I didn't need my clippers, I plugged them in to make sure they weren't damaged after they had hit the floor. Uh-oh, no welcoming buzz, no vibration—dead!

I radioed the office. "Jan to Base. Lois, my clippers broke. I think you'll have to cancel the rest of my appointments. Over."

"Jan, Niel just came in, says he left work early because his carpool wanted to go home. Snow's predicted, you know. Do you want me to ask him to bring you another clipper?"

Snow? I hadn't heard anything about snow this morning.

"Ah, yeah, thanks."

My long-suffering husband agreed, bless him, and in a somewhat better mood, I returned Pedro to Mr. Warner. I fixed my most gracious smile to my face as I pointed out to him the snappy scarf around his pup's neck. Mr. Warner wasn't buying it. He huffed, handed me some crumpled bills, and when he banged the door shut, I felt its wind whistle past my face.

Backing out of the alley, I scraped a utility pole and was in danger of snapping back to my previously grouchy self. But I could get along without my right-side mirror, which was now cracked, if I were very, very careful and hugged the beltway's outside lane.

My next customer was a repeat, and I had no problem finding her home. Niel met me and everything was hunky-dory until I rang Mrs. Perry's doorbell and spotted a note tacked to her door. "Jan, I'm so sorry, schools are closing and I had to run over to pick up Mary. Your phone was busy, so I couldn't get hold of you. I'll call and reschedule."

All right! As far as I was concerned, this was good news. I had just caught up on my schedule. In fact, I was now running ahead. I moseyed back to my van and noticed the sky was grey with low-lying clouds. A few snowflakes floated down. I mused, "How pretty."

I had Lois phone Customer Number Four to tell her I was running ahead of schedule.

"Base to Jan. No one answered. I left a message that you were running early and would get there around 11:30. Over."

"OK, if she's not home when I arrive, I'll grab a sandwich somewhere."

Sandy wasn't there when I pulled up, but by this time, I knew where every fast food joint was located. I turned around and headed to a Burger King. With lunch nestled on the passenger's seat, I drove back and parked. Mesmerized, I watched the light, wispy snow fall as I munched on a Whopper. I decided to call it a day and started up the van.

Just as I threw my lunch wrappings into the trash, ready to head back to Base, Sandy, frantically waving at me, zipped into her driveway.

"I'm here. I'm here," she shouted to me, dashed into her house, and brought out Spaz, a large springer spaniel. As I lifted him to the table, Spaz lived up to his name. With all four legs scrambling, he knocked over my super-sized drink and soaked my beige smock. Fortunately, it was a clear Sprite and although drenched, I was not Coke brown.

At the end of Spaz's grooming, we were both worn out. He had nipped at the brush and wound up with bristles in his nose. When I sprayed him, he snapped at the water. I knew better than to try to blow-dry him. In the past he'd gone berserk and tried to eat the dryer. I didn't mind. That allowed me to towel dry him and save some time. He was a good old boy, just a bit of a "Spaz."

Back in the van, I checked my next appointment. Doggie Number Five was new, a Lhasa apso named Sally. I was always apprehensive about grooming a new dog and as I read her record, I noted the owner mentioned Sally was a bit skittish. Did "skittish" mean she bites? My radar was up, and I considered returning to Base and calling it a day, but since the snow wasn't sticking, I decided to continue.

Uh-oh. The engine wouldn't start. I turned the starter again and again until it made that horrible grinding sound. I radioed Base and bypassing Lois, spoke directly to my spouse, who had just arrived back.

"Niel, the van won't start. Can you meet me here and see if you can get it going? Oh, and would you tell Lois to phone my fifth and tell them I'll call as soon as I get going?"

Peeved that the little time I made up earlier was rapidly disappearing, I finished off my Sprite, and boned up on Lhasa grooming.

Niel arrived within half an hour, attached jumper cables and—varoom! The van started.

Niel asked, "Why are your lights on?"

"Headlights?" Oh, dear. I'd run the battery down. I was sure I'd hear more about this little episode later.

I made it without incident to my next appointment and remembered to turn off my lights. Snow was beginning to cover my hood. Slipping and sliding, I gingerly made my way to the front door.

Mrs. Backus didn't even say hello. She started in, "Is your van warm? Is the water heated? I don't want my Sally out there if it's cold."

I guaranteed that my van was toasty and the water temperature perfect for her darling Lhasa apso.

Only then did Mrs. Backus give me extensive grooming instructions for Sally. Since it's impossible to groom a damp, snow-flaked dog, I decided to cover Sally with my coat and carry her to the van so she wouldn't get wet. I picked her up, and Sally, true to her ancient guard dog breed, bit me. I yelped. She yelped. Mrs. Backus yelped. And just in case her message hadn't registered, Sally bit me again.

Mrs. Backus pulled Sally from my arms and said, "She doesn't like you!"

The feeling was mutual, but trying to salvage the appointment, I placated her. "Most dogs don't like strangers picking them up in their own homes. Probably nothing to do with me, but since she might bite again, would you mind carrying her to the van?"

Mrs. Backus glanced behind me; I turned around, too. How did the snow accumulate so quickly? Whew. There were about two inches on the ground, and for Baltimore, that was a major snowfall.

She said, "I think I'd better reschedule. I don't want Sally out in this snow."

Out in this snow? Sally was going to be in my cozy van, but I couldn't convince Mrs. Backus to keep the appointment.

It was time to head home, but when I entered the "on" ramp of the beltway, I was dismayed to see vehicles abandoned on the shoulder. It wasn't going to be an easy drive. I prayed, "God, get me home safely," and hoped He was paying attention. Besides, wasn't he in charge of "weather?" He couldn't have timed a snow event on an "off" day?

I radioed, "Jan to Base. I'm on my way in, Lois."

Niel radioed back, "Lois left an hour ago. Watch it driving back."

By the time I made it home, my shoulders were cramped with tension. My back ached from leaning forward to see the road, and when I finally pulled into the driveway, I had to pry my hands from the steering wheel.

Niel greeted me at the door with the report that the phone was continually ringing, and there might be more than twenty messages on the answering machine. He added, "Yep, I think I overheard several customers canceling appointments for tomorrow." He was way too cheerful, and I figured this was the beginning of payback for having to bail me out twice.

Anyway, my day was over, and I traded in my soaked shoes for a pair of comfy slippers. My still annoyed (but supportive) spouse heated a cup of cocoa for me and after resting a bit, I totaled my receipts and tackled those pesky phone messages. I had groomed three dogs, had one no-show, and received two dog bites that fortunately were tiny and didn't require stitches—all in a day's work.

6

The Lion Clip

"Confessions of a Mobile Pet Groomer" would suggest I have secrets.

I do. And one is that I don't know much about cats. Not that I don't like cats, it's just that I didn't know many. The only cats in my life arrived when a neighbor threatened to haul a mother cat, which had the nerve to deliver a passel of kittens in her flower bed, off to the pound.

"Mom," our kids chorused, "we've got to rescue them!" and rounded them up in the dead of night.

Mama cat took off, and a lucky thing, too. She probably sensed our neighbor was serious about that "pound" thing.

We managed to con friends into taking two, but the last one, Chessie (yes, the same cat that terrorized our secretary), lived with us for twenty years. Although a tiny kitten, he had already spent too much time in the wild, and never really adapted to domesticity. He inhabited our basement and favored us with his presence only at feeding time. Some pet!

Since Chessie was the extent of my "hands on" cat experience, I anticipated I would learn how to handle and groom them in school.

Not so.

During the entire twelve-week course only six cats were dropped off. I was already stressed out because I hadn't passed my schnauzer test and now it looked like I wasn't going to learn diddly-squat about grooming cats.

But during the last week of school, Tanya dropped one on my grooming table, said, "Here's yours," and walked away.

I called to her, "Uh, what do I do?"

"Hon, whatever he'll let you."

Sammy, a short-haired brown, black and white tabby cat, appeared quite docile as he yawned and stretched out on my table. I eyed him and said to Tanya's back, "All I have to do is brush him out, trim nails, clean ears, bathe and put him in a cage to dry, right?

"That's it," she bellowed from across the room.

I reached over to pet Sammy and he reached right back, except his reach included a set of sharp nails that clawed the back of my hand.

"Ow-wee!"

I decided right then and there that since Sammy was short-haired and didn't need brushing, I'd just trim his nails and shampoo him. I picked up my nail-clipper and Sammy hissed. I backed right off. I had no clue how to go about doing this. Flipping through my notebook to check whether I had scribbled something about trimming nails on uncooperative animals, I found only one sure-fire suggestion: put a leash around his neck. I was pretty sure I couldn't do that with Sammy—he'd probably jump off the table and strangle himself.

"Hey, I need some guidance over here," I shouted to Tanya.

"Use the cat muzzle," she shouted back.

Cat muzzle? What did that look like?

I pawed through the school's supplies and pulled out what I hoped was a cat muzzle. Getting it on Sammy's head, however, was no easy thing. A fellow student came over and between her holding him in a vise grip and me slipping the muzzle over his head, we had him secured enough to snip his lethal claws.

Ready to bathe him, I put a mesh kitty bag on him so that just his head and tail poked out. That way, if he tried to claw me, he wouldn't be able to get those wicked nails through the netting, and I could spray him down and shampoo him while he was encased in it. I gave a silent "thank you" to the inventor of that marvelous piece of webbing.

As soon as the water sprayed over him he started to howl, and kept it up until the end. I wasn't loving this process either and wanted to howl along with him. Afterward, I placed him in a cage and aimed heavy-duty driers at him. I was going to finish his grooming by brushing him out after all (if he'd let me), but I didn't have to. When I removed him from the drying cage, all his loose hair had been blown off.

Since my first catgrooming experience hadn't been exactly a stellar success, it stood to reason that when Canine Clippers got going, I was leery of felines. In retrospect, maybe I named the company "Canine…" because of my trepidation of booking cats for grooming. But I wanted to capture as many customers as possible to pump up my business and put a second van on the road, so schedule them I did, and my cat grooming education expanded along with my share of scratches and bites.

The first cat I groomed in my van, Lily, was a delightful, long-haired Persian that purred while I brushed her out and trimmed her nails. We developed a real relationship and I revised my negative opinion—until I placed her in the tub and turned on the spray. As the first few drops hit her, she jumped from the tub and landed on my chest.

I cuddled her, cooing, "It's OK, Lily, I know. It's just water. You'll be all right."

She climbed up to my neck and dug in for a better grip. Her claws raked my shoulder and when I attempted to pull her away, she burrowed deeper. No way could I pry her loose. When I tried, she just inched higher until she was over my shoulder and halfway down my back. Ouch!

She and I remained locked in position for several seconds while I weighed my options on how to solve this impasse. Lily gave up first, and withdrawing her claws, jumped back to the table. Relieved, I cast aside the mental image of the creature in the movie *Alien* permanently attached to my body.

Lily did not receive a bath that day, but I did; I gingerly washed out my battle wounds (one of the perks of having water, soap and peroxide stocked in the van). To add insult to injury, her owner refused to pay me for the aborted grooming.

During that first half-year I learned that most dogs warned you when they were unhappy. They yawned, licked their chops, shifted, growled and finally, if you stupidly ignored those signals, they attacked.

Cats? No warning. Some turned into raging Tasmanian devils, sinking their claws or fangs into my tender hand. Normally, a little bite wasn't a problem unless that hand ballooned to monstrous proportions. Panic set in when red streaks, indicating blood poisoning, ran up my arm. A cat bite generally resulted in a loss of income for a minimum of three days—not to mention the pain. Nope. Cats weren't for me.

In time, I reached the conclusion that there were enough dirty dogs out there to sustain my business, and I didn't have to deal with cats. Eventually I made a few rules for myself and I share them here with you for your enlightenment as well:

- Rule Number One: Do not trust cats. They'll lull you into thinking they're docile, and just when you lower your guard, all hell breaks loose.

- Rule Number Two: Always keep antiseptic and Band-Aids at hand. The odds are that kitty will make sure you require them.

- Rule Number Three: Don't try to go solo. Grooming a cat frequently requires another pair of hands.

- Rule Number Four: Don't schedule any cat appointments, and if you do, cancel it as soon as you come to your senses.

Regretfully, I didn't always stick to Rule Number Four.

Dismayed when I noticed a cat on my itinerary one morning, I asked my secretary, "Who scheduled this cat?"

"Oh, you mean Tiger?" she said with an air of innocence. "The owner specifically asked for you."

Against my better judgment, I decided to keep the appointment, but I told her to never add another one. Checking Tiger's file I spotted one cautionary remark his owner had offered. "He's one sneaky cat."

Uh-oh, bad vibes.

On the drive there, I told myself that one false move out of Tiger and he was going back in the house, even if it meant forfeiting my fee. Pondering his name added to my anxiety. Did it reflect his appearance or his personality? I hoped for the former.

When I arrived, I was delighted to see Tiger had stripes, but still there was that ominous note from his owner about "sneaky." I brushed him out, cleaned his ears and trimmed his nails. He didn't move; not one twitch. Obviously, he was just biding his time. I bathed and blow-dried him, still nothing. My neck muscles were tense and I was edgy, ready to back off if I saw the slightest indication of an unhappy kitty.

I picked up my ten-inch, beautifully honed scissors to trim a few final hairs, and had them halfway to his body when he opened his jaws as far as they would go. At the sight of Tiger's spiky teeth, I flinched and jerked the scissors upward, driving them into the middle of my forehead.

Holy cow! Blood gushed from the wound and into my eyes. I groped, half-blind, for Tiger, and fumbled for the horn in hopes of catching his owner's attention.

She flung open the van door and shrieked, "Oh, my God! Did Tiger do that to you?"

"No! Please just grab him and guide me to the house."

She collected her cat while I snatched a grooming towel to staunch the flow of blood.

I clutched the owner's shirttail and had her lead me back to her home where I cleaned my neatly pierced forehead.

"I'm so sorry. I'm so sorry," Tiger's owner said over and over as she bandaged my wound.

"It's not his fault," I kept telling her. "I'll be fine."

Tiger hadn't done a thing but yawn. He didn't need to.

As I left the house, Tiger was lying on the sofa purring and content with a definite smirk on his face. I, however, much less content, raced to the emergency room for a tetanus shot. Although he had been successfully groomed, we both knew who had won.

After that, you would have thought I'd pay more attention to Rule Number Four. But, no, I ignored it. Just like the Bibilical Eve, I succumbed to flattery when Mrs. Perry pleaded, "Jan, you do such a beautiful job with Skippy. I know Kitty will give you no trouble."

What was I thinking when I said, "Oh, I'd love to!" Why did I have such a penchant for wanting to please?

The dreaded day arrived. I groused at my foolhardy scheduling while driving to Mrs. Perry's home. I vaguely remembered her grey, thick-coated, medium-sized cat from the few times I had seen her when I groomed Skippy, but knew nothing about Kitty's personality.

When Mrs. Perry met me at the door, she had Kitty nestled in her arms, eyes half-closed with her motor running big-time. Since her owner had her wrapped in a blanket, I couldn't get a good look at her.

Mrs. Perry followed me and as she stepped into my rolling grooming parlor, she asked, "So what's my job here?"

"I may need your help holding her during the grooming. Sometimes this turns into a two-person job. Just put her on the table and be ready to step in when I need you."

Experience told me she was clueless about what was about to happen. Mrs. Perry presumed she would simply sit and watch. Discovering otherwise pretty quickly, she wasn't too sure about her decision to help out.

Kitty narrowed her eyes and flattened her body on the grooming table. A twitch traveled from her neck to her rear. No doubt recognizing doggie odors, she'd surmised that this van was not a feline spa.

Kitty was not happy. Kitty stopped purring. Kitty stiffened, arched her back and hissed.

Mrs. Perry reached for Kitty, held her tighter and squeaked, "I don't think she likes this!"

I was positive Kitty didn't like this, but that never stopped me from completing a grooming. I evaluated her condition. She had chewed her fur into one huge grey mat from head to rear.

"Mrs. Perry, I'm afraid I'm going to have to shave Kitty."

"Oh, isn't she going to look strange? Won't that hurt?" Her enthusiasm was rapidly waning.

It was time I gave her the worst case scenario. To avoid aftershock, I said in my most professional voice, "I'll do my best to save the fur on her head and tail. We call it 'The Lion Clip.'"

I watched Kitty's owner mull this information over, visualizing what her darling pet might look like. Hesitantly, she said, "Oh, that might be cute."

Before she had time to reconsider, I said, "Well, it's time to begin. Hold Kitty with one hand around her neck, and with your other, get a firm grip near her tail."

Hoping to accustom her pet to the buzzing, I reached for my clipper, turned it on and waved it near Kitty's body. Mrs. Perry might have been oblivious that the skirmish was about to begin, but Kitty wasn't. Her ears flattened, her tail waved to and fro, and the hiss turned into a growl.

Just then, Mrs. Perry's cell phone rang. She removed one hand from Kitty's neck to answer the call, and her cat seized the diversion to launch herself into a flying leap. Landing on her mistress' shoulder, she dug her claws in for a better grip.

Mrs. Perry shouted, "Help! Oh my God! Get her off me!"

I tried to remove Kitty's claws from her owner's body while simultaneously avoiding the cat's sharp teeth. Having no luck, I firmly gripped her body near her tail with both hands and dragged her from the client's shredded blouse and raked shoulder. Mrs. Perry, sobbing and hiccupping, dabbed at her blood-streaked clothing while I returned Kitty to the grooming table. Kitty's growl turned into a snarl, and I knew her owner would be of no further help *whatsoever*.

"You know," I advised, "I think I can handle Kitty myself. Why don't you go back in and return your call. I'll yell if I need you."

"Oh, thank you!" she said as she scurried from the van, no longer a willing assistant.

I shut the van door and faced Kitty, "It's just you and me now."

Ding—Round One. I eyeballed Kitty. Kitty glared back. I grasped her with one hand and reached for the clipper with the other. She had been waiting for this opportunity, broke away from my grip, jumped from the table and landed on the van's front seat. As I reached for her, she bounded onto the floor and shot to the rear. We played ring-around-the-van for a few minutes until she aimed for a high shelf in the back and sprung onto it. The clever puss spun around and backed into the far reaches of the corner where I couldn't tackle her without encountering her fangs.

I terminated the chase and imagined Kitty was celebrating, "I've won the battle." Ha! Not on her life.

I had wasted thirty minutes attempting to get my clipper near Kitty and I wasn't capitulating. Quoting the groomer's mantra, I muttered, "I will not leave here without money!"

Ding—Round Two. Grabbing a noose in one hand and a broom in the other, I attempted to dislodge her from her sanctuary. The hisses and growls escalated into yowls. I shoved the broom at her. She punched back with a fast right and a left. I feared Mrs. Perry might hear the battle, but figured she was probably preoccupied with dressing her wounds.

Neither Kitty nor I were ready to throw in the towel, but I realized there was no way I could groom this cat without help. We were at a stand-off. While I considered my options, she spotted the air vent on the van's ceiling. She rocketed over my head to freedom—a brilliant maneuver—except that her front claws caught in the vent's screen. As she hung there, stretched out and amazed at her predicament, she stopped yowling. I was equally amazed, but swiftly counter-attacked by pushing her rear claws into the screening. Now I had Kitty captive, hanging upside down by all fours. The advantage was mine!

Ding—Round Three. Although I hadn't been taught how to shave a topsy-turvy animal, I realized that whatever method I used, it had to be quick. I switched on my clippers and speedily shaved Kitty's back while she was conveniently indisposed. I even managed to angle my clipper to cut the fur off her without leaving nicks and gouges. It wasn't the smoothest of clips, but as we groomers told each other when confronted with a difficult animal, "It's a best-you-can-do job."

I threw a mesh kitty bag over her, and unhooked those sharp claws, one by one, from the screen. I then placed Kitty in the tub, shampooed and rinsed her. No way was I going to even attempt aiming a hair dryer at her—it would have driven her completely berserk. I patted her dry, spritzed some cologne and sprinted back to the house with my victim securely wrapped in a towel.

It was a blessing that Mrs. Perry would be unaware of her cherished pet's unorthodox grooming. Certain she was expecting a purring, adorable, dried ball of fluff, I was apprehensive as I entered her home.

Kitty played the role of a drowned but clean cat. For my part, I acted as though nothing out of the ordinary had taken place. I placed a wet, vanquished pet into her owner's arms. In a funk, Kitty leaped from Mrs. Perry's grasp, sprang to the couch and began grooming her absent fur.

Mrs. Perry, obviously nearsighted, said, "Doesn't she look cute!" For heaven's sake, didn't she notice Kitty was sopping wet? Handing me a check, she asked, "Did she give you any trouble?"

"Nah," I assured her with a smile, making a mental note to never again schedule this animal for a grooming.

7

The Gypsy Groomer

I congratulated myself that Canine Clippers had grown so fast that within six months a second van was almost roadworthy. Lenny was just putting the finishing touches on it. Yes, it was Lenny again. He hadn't exactly done a bang-up job constructing our first van—but he was the only game in town.

I placed an ad in *The Baltimore Sun*, but this time it was for a groomer, and not office help. The ad had been in for more than two weeks and Bonnie was the first one to respond. I would remember this later when hiring other groomers—not to expect immediate responses. It would take weeks to get anyone to answer my ad. Apparently, they found working in a van, dealing with clients and having the vans break down on their route much too challenging. But Bonnie was up for the challenge—or was she?

There she sat: skinny, with long dark hair, and a short, short skirt. A form-fitting sweater, boots and feather earrings completed her Woodstock get-up. In her whispery, hopeful voice Bonnie said, "I've had lots of grooming experience."

"Great," I said, smiling. "Why don't you fill out this application and then we'll talk."

She took the application, swiveled to face the other desk in our tiny office and mulled over the questionnaire. During the next hour I fielded phone calls and confirmed appointments while she labored over the simple one-page application. Tentatively, she handed it back. I looked it over and couldn't help spotting crossed out answers and teensy, weensy explanations in the margins. Upon closer examination her replies to questions were ambiguous and confusing. Either she had a poor memory, or she was writing misleading or untruthful responses. Her application indicated several decades of experience as a pet groomer. This gal was older than her twenty-something hippie appearance suggested.

Pasty faced, and with her pallid skin stretched over protruding arm and leg bones, she appeared frail, unhealthy and ready to fall over if bumped. I questioned whether she had the stamina to groom. Except for her mass of thick, long curls, her appearance was that of a Holocaust survivor. But since she was the only person who had answered my ad, and I was eager to man Van Number Two, I reluctantly hired quirky Bonnie.

During the first week she arrived late three out of the five days. Her excuses were the usual ones, "My alarm didn't go off," "My car wouldn't start," or "Traffic was really heavy and I didn't want to get off the expressway to find a pay phone." The most original was, "My cat knocked the alarm clock off my nightstand." (Creativity: A. Punctuality: F).

My Type A personality clashed with Bonnie's Type B. Over time, I discovered Bonnie had many far-fetched reasons why she didn't arrive on time, and each one irked me.

Directionally challenged, north, south, east and west were meaningless to her. I discovered she mapped her way around Baltimore by writing directions using "left" or "right" routing. Bonnie radioed in when she lost her way, and I'd direct her street-by-street until she located the home.

"I found it, I found it!" she said while the radio snapped, crackled and popped with her nervous laughter.

Once she had an appointment near downtown Baltimore and was fifteen miles outside the city, and heading toward the mountains of Western Maryland before she realized her error.

Trying to assist her one day, I asked, "Would a compass mounted on the dash help you?"

She shrugged. We installed one anyway. It didn't help.

But if Bonnie, a Baltimore native, was able to locate a main street near the client's home, she generally found her way there—late. Once there, she took nearly twice as long to groom a dog than she should have.

Mrs. Burns phoned, "Jan, Bonnie is still out in the van with Buster. Do you think something happened?"

"Let me radio her and check what's taking so long."

"Base to Bonnie. Over."

"Bonnie here."

"Bonnie, Mrs. Burns said it's taking a long time to groom Buster. Is there a problem?"

"Oh, no. He and I are getting along just fine. I should have him done in about another half hour. Clear"

I phoned her client back, "Mrs. Burns, Bonnie said she'd have Buster in soon. If this is a problem for you, I can groom him myself in the future."

"Oh, no. I wouldn't dream of having him groomed by anyone else. He loves Bonnie."

Although many of Bonnie's customers complained about the excessive amount of time it took her to finish their dogs, they always raved about the quality of her work, and in the end, made allowances for her. After all, it was their beloved pet receiving an exceptional, careful grooming. Right?

As a result of Bonnie's terminal case of the "slows" (Baltimoreans' name for habitually tardy citizens), she usually pulled into Base around six or seven in the evening. Not only did I worry, but her tardy arrivals interfered with my precious evening hours. It was not unusual for me to phone her last customer to find out when she had left. Often she was still there, sometimes grooming, sometimes visiting, but always taking her good old time.

In the end, I adjusted her grooming appointments from one hour to an hour and a half, plus travel—but to no avail. The more time I gave Bonnie, the more time she took. One evening when she was particularly late, I phoned her last customer, "Is Bonnie still groom-ing Chico?"

"Oh my, no! Bonnie left here several hours ago."

I tried to reach her on the radio—no answer.

Around 9:30, I heard her pulling into the driveway and rushed out to meet her, "Bonnie, where have you been?"

"Mmm, I got a really good tip from my last customer, so I stopped at the bingo parlor."

Peeved, but also relieved, I said, "I tried radioing you, but you didn't answer. I was very concerned that you'd had an accident!"

"Sorry about that."

It wasn't the only time I wondered where she was with my van. Bonnie habitually grocery shopped, stopped at flea markets and searched for bargains at the mall after grooming her last dog for the day. Her life was her job, and she all but lived in that van. To relieve my anxiety, I asked her to contact me if she wasn't coming in directly after her last appointment. Ultimately, I gave up trying to control Bonnie's hours.

She liked to decorate her surroundings with comfy objects. If I had to groom in her van, it meant listening to the "tinkle, tinkle" of chimes and ducking rubber animals, dream chasers and charms dangling from the ceiling.

I told her, "Bonnie, your van doesn't look very professional. Please tidy up and remove some of the trinkets."

For a brief while, she stashed them under the passenger seat, but, like the bunny in the magician's hat, they'd always reappear.

Bonnie's van-cleaning methods were questionable, too. I followed an efficient routine and attempted to train her to do the same.

"Bonnie, I suggest that when you come in at night and while the van is filling with water, you bring in your dirty towels, gather fresh ones and count your receipts. You should be finished by the time your tank is filled. The entire process would be over in five minutes—flat."

My advice didn't work. Her routine went more like: Van pulled into driveway, no sign of life for twenty minutes. What was she doing out there? When she sauntered in, the water was not turned on, and the dirty towels were still comfortably nestled in their bin. She began counting her money, but realizing she hadn't started the water, she abandoned totaling her cash, and hurried back out. She turned it on full force and satisfied it was gushing into the tank, she traipsed back to the office—still minus the towels. Her attention focused again on attempting to match cash to receipts.

Frustrated with the process, she'd phone a friend, follow up with a trip to the bathroom, and then check out our medicine cabinet. Meanwhile, water would be pouring out of the filler tube and onto the driveway (think winter, think ice, think slipping, think broken bones, think worker's compensation claim). Relaxing in the bathroom, Bonnie was oblivious to Niagara Falls outside.

I knocked on the door and yelled, "Bonnie, your water is overflowing and running down the driveway!"

"Oh, my gosh, I'll get it!" She moseyed out to the van and returned—sans towels.

The counting continued until finally she threw the cash and receipts on my desk. She said, "My money doesn't come out. I don't know what's wrong."

"Can you match the checks to the receipts as a beginning?"

"I'll try that."

A few minutes later she piped up, "I think I lost a check. I'll have to search the van. Maybe I put it in my grooming case." The hunt was on until she fished the missing check from out of her empty drink cup. In response to my frown, she said, "It's just a tad damp, not bad, you can still read the amount—ink hasn't run yet."

Did her money match her receipts? No, of course not. Throwing her hands up in the air and in an aggrieved voice, she complained, "My money never comes out for me. I'll just put everything in the envelope and maybe you can figure it out!"

If she lucked out and I was absent from the office, she eliminated the charade of at least *attempting* to have her money and receipts match. She plunked the entire kit and caboodle into a packet and scooted out before I caught her. Bless her. She thought she was finished and her problem was now my problem.

I coached, "Bonnie, did you bring your towels in?" and added, "Have you closed all the windows, locked the van, and turned the water heater, furnace (or A/C) and water pump off?"

At first, I was amused with Bonnie's method of organizing her grooming equipment. She didn't actually have a grooming case. She chucked all of her tools into a canvas sack which also held a jumble of food, drinks and cash. It wasn't unusual for liquids to spill on her grooming equipment, and she'd borrow mine until she saved enough to pay for repairing her scissors and blades. I became less amused when I ended up loaning her money to purchase more equipment. She never seemed to have enough to live on and frequently asked for an advance on her pay.

Lucky for Bonnie, she had several redeeming qualities. Otherwise, her tardiness and hoarding natures would have gotten her fired. Bonnie's love for animals was amazing and her grooming was beautiful. She truly wanted each pet to bond with her, and they did. Her customers adored her, and she had many who routinely requested her services. I finally decided that if they didn't mind her taking an abnormally long time to groom their pets, why should I? As long as she finished six dogs a day—fine with me.

One day I received a call from Mrs. Hardy. "The groomer isn't here yet."

"Let me see if I can get hold of her and get an estimate as to when she expects to arrive."

I tried to reach Bonnie by two-way radio. She didn't respond. I called Mrs. Hardy back and said I would contact her as soon as I reached Bonnie. I phoned her previous customer to see if she was still there or, more optimistically, when she had left.

Imagine my astonishment when she said, "Oh, Bonnie left here about forty-five minutes ago. She is such a nice girl, and little Pongo looks so good. She sure takes her time with him."

Yep, I knew that! But where was she now? If she left forty-five minutes ago, she should have arrived at Mrs. Hardy's in fifteen minutes. I phoned Mrs. Hardy to see if, in the interim, Bonnie had arrived.

Mrs. Hardy was understandbly testy. "No, she hasn't and I have to leave here shortly."

I apologized. "If it's convenient when you arrive back home, please phone me and I'll come right out and groom your pup." I phoned the customer scheduled after Mrs. Hardy to see if she could have Bonnie call in when she arrived.

I was surprised when she said, "Oh, Bonnie's here now. She's been working on Pansy for at least half an hour."

"Well, would you please have her call the office when she brings Pansy back in?"

"Sure will. She is such a pleasant person. Pansy really likes her."

"Yes, I know, I know." My patience was floundering.

Finally, Bonnie called in, "What's up?"

"Bonnie, Mrs. Hardy says you missed her appointment to groom Frank. What happened?"

Puzzled, she said, "I groomed her dog. She has a white Westie, right?"

"Yes, she does, but she says you never showed up."

It was my turn to be confused. I quickly phoned Mrs. Hardy, who hadn't quite made it out the door, and she insisted Bonnie hadn't arrived. Hmm. I switched to detective mode. "Could you describe your home, Mrs. Hardy?"

"I have a white colonial."

"How about your neighbors' homes on either side of you, and also, do you know if either of them also owns a Westie?"

"Well, there's a ranch with a long driveway to our south and they have one." She shared their name and phone number with me.

I phoned Pansy's owner again and asked her if Bonnie was still there. Of course, she was! Why wouldn't she be?

"Bonnie, would you describe the house where you groomed the Westie?"

"I think it was a brick ranch."

"Bonnie, you went to the wrong house!"

She argued. "I don't *think* so. The owner said the dog looked great and paid me. She even gave me a nice tip. Why would a stranger do that?"

Why indeed?

I phoned Mrs. Hardy's neighbor. An elderly lady with a shaky voice answered.

"Hi, Mrs. Cormand? This is Jan from Canine Clippers. Did one of our groomers groom your Westie today?"

"Well this isn't Mrs. Cormand, this is her mother. But, yes, the groomer left some time back. It was a surprise to me when she showed up. Usually my daughter tells me when someone is coming to the house. She did do a lovely job though, if that's what you're asking about, although we don't generally pay that much to have Chucky groomed."

Aha! Perhaps I should have considered a career as a sleuth. I advised her I'd call her daughter later to discuss the misunderstanding.

When Bonnie came in that evening, she didn't seem one bit perturbed that she had gone to the wrong house, much less groomed some-one else's dog.

"Oh, isn't that funny," she giggled.

I was *not* amused! I had spent my entire evening grooming her missed dog. But Bonnie was unconcerned. She just figured everyone was happy—Bonnie certainly was.

Misreading house numbers continued to be a problem for her. It wouldn't be the only time she got lost or rang the wrong doorbell, but it was the last time she groomed the wrong dog.

Bonnie had been with us for five years when she became pregnant. She decided to marry the father. During her fourth month, she became violently ill with morning sickness and was forced to resign. Other than a birth announcement, we didn't hear from Bonnie for another five years. When we did, she was in the middle of a nasty divorce, and her husband had custody of their son. She needed a job. Since we were one groomer short, we rehired her.

Why? Why? Why? Bonnie's old quirks resurfaced in no time, along with new ones she had picked up in the intervening years. Her fellow groomers complained that our towel shelf in the basement was always bare. I checked Bonnie's van, and sure enough, she had sixty or so towels stashed away instead of the twelve to fifteen generally needed. In addition, she stockpiled her van with twice the shampoos, colognes and other miscellaneous grooming supplies. She simply couldn't bear an empty shelf or nook in her van.

How had we forgotten she was a pack rat? Beads, feathers, clothes, candy, pictures and food were squirreled away. Chimes tinkled and photos of her son dangled from the ceiling. Traveling gypsies kept a neater wagon. Sometimes I wondered why she didn't purchase an air mattress, sleep in the van and avoid paying rent.

Cigarette butts filled the ashtray. Whoa! There were cigarette butts? We had a standing rule that employees could not smoke in the vans. Not only were some pets and their owners allergic to smoke, but so were a few fellow groomers who occasionally had to work in her van.

I cautioned, "Bonnie, we're receiving complaints from customers who say their dogs smell like smoke when they're brought in. You cannot smoke in the van! If you must have a cigarette, stop and get out to light up."

Bonnie continued puffing away in the van. The only noticeable change was the increased level of wafting incense. She would not, could not, stop smoking. Air deodorizers joined the incense, and an atmospheric battle raged among the three. I advised her that if customers continued to complain, her job would be in jeopardy.

I hesitated to fire this talented, loving, skilled, but unorganized, tardy, smoking groomer. However, we were also dealing with a disobedient employee who wasn't a good role model for others. The issue came to a head after the Christmas rush in a manner I couldn't have predicted.

"Jan," she announced, "I have a doctor's appointment during Christmas break. I think I have hemorrhoids."

I resolved to discuss the smoking issue after the holiday.

But that was the last time we saw Bonnie. She was diagnosed with cancer. Her customers missed her, sent get-well cards and kept in touch with her. When one of our other employees groomed a dog that had been hers, the owners always asked how Bonnie was faring. Sometimes they gave the groomer an envelope with a money gift for her.

Amazingly, she recovered and went on to finish nursing school, which she had begun many years previously. We stayed in touch by phone. One day she said she might have a wee problem passing her physics course.

Recalling her difficulty counting receipts, I said, "Bonnie, if you have to add or subtract, yes, I think you're going to have a tough time."

She giggled and I wished her well, my Gypsy groomer.

8

Orphan Pets

My first experience with pets abandoned by their owners occurred when I was still in grooming school. Rambo was one of the first dogs assigned to me and since he was a shorthaired mixed-breed, he didn't require much in the way of grooming. Rambo was one of those dogs which, thank goodness, didn't live up to his name. He was good-natured about being brushed, having his nails clipped, and he didn't try to climb out of the bathtub. He was ready to be retrieved by his owner, but by 5:00, when most pets were long gone, he was still in his cage—waiting. And so were we.

Tanya punched in the phone number from Rambo's file and the mechanical voice coming through the speaker said, "The number you dialed is no longer in service."

She nodded to the class and announced, "When this happens you have to stay until he's picked up and don't forget to charge a kennel fee."

We sneaked a few glances at each other and mouthed, "Stay late? Not me." Was Tanya going to coerce us into drawing straws for dog sitting? This was going beyond what we'd signed up for. Not only did the grooming school receive our tuition, but also collected fees from its customers (with no discount for inexperienced students working on their pets). Was she also going to take advantage of our presence for other assigned duties? Talk about exploitation!

Around 6:00 she made a decision. "OK, I'll put him back in the kennel, and we'll see if he gets picked up in the morning."

Relieved we weren't playing groomer roulette to see who was going to bunk down in the salon, we sprinted for the door before she changed her mind.

When I arrived the following morning, Rambo was still in a kennel. Tanya informed us this wasn't the first occasion someone dropped off a dog and never came back. She puckered her mouth and confronted us. "Which one of you wants to take this dog home?"

Did I hear that right? Was this part of the school's training—all leftover dogs went home with students? What did my contract say about this?

No one offered to be the orphan's new owner. Who among us needed another dog? Absent was the usual bantering as we mulled over this sweet abandoned dog's fate throughout the day.

Tanya closed up shop, and because no one had volunteered to be Rambo's new owner, she uttered the magic words she knew would touch a sympathetic nerve, "One of you can drop him off at the dog pound on your way home."

Was she serious? She knew exactly the response that announcement would trigger in our animal-loving souls. Thank God another student offered to take Rambo and the rest of us were off the hook.

I smugly reassured myself that this predicament would never occur in my mobile grooming business. I knew exactly where my dog owners lived—I parked in their driveways after all, and I would always, after the final spray of cologne, deliver my charges right back to their homes. No problem, right?

One day after I had been bouncing along the streets of Baltimore for a year or so, I arrived at the home of one of my favorite customers, eighty-year-old Mrs. Crandle.

In a quavering voice she said, "Jan, can you take Twinkles? I'm moving to an assisted living facility next week. I'm heartbroken that I can't take her with me. I'm so afraid she'll be put down."

She was teary-eyed and my eyes dampened with sympathy for her. I had groomed Twinkles, her adorable shih tzu, for almost a year and had developed a close relationship with both her and Mrs. Crandle. I was well aware that Twinkle's future looked gloomy—at age twelve and having lost an eye, she also suffered from arthritis. Who out there in their right minds would adopt a geriatric pet with medical problems? I was Mrs. Crandle's last hope, but I couldn't take in every homeless dog.

I drove Twinkles to a "no-kill" shelter where Mrs. Crandle paid a small amount toward her room and board each month until another home was found for her. I asked the shelter manager to stay in touch with me, but I wasn't optimistic about Twinkle's chances. Much to my surprise, about a month later I received a call from the shelter. A retired gentleman who worked there part-time, had recently lost his dog and fallen in love with Twinkles.

The shelter had given him my business card and after adopting her, he contacted me. I continued grooming Twinkles for several more years, and he later told me, "I'm so glad Twinkles and I found each other. We're spending our twilight years together."

Every few months Mrs. Crandle and I went for an outing and visited Twinkles. It was the best of endings, but many others did not end so happily.

It became obvious that the longer I groomed pets, the more I needed a file of shelters where orphaned or unwanted animals were cared for until they were adopted or died. These facilities, staffed by concerned dog and cat lovers, made it their mission to save every pet they could. Sometimes there was a fee, sometimes not. At the very least, these facilities provided a solution for owners no longer able to care for their beloved friends.

Almost every type of dog—greyhounds, cocker spaniels and even pit bulls—had rescue groups devoted to finding homes for their particular breed. But what about those Heinz 57 Varieties? If they were dropped off at the pound and weren't adopted within a certain amount of time, they were euthanized. I was bothered by the huge number of pups out there that needed homes.

Unwanted pets were routinely dropped off at our home. The business had grown to five hard-to-miss vans parked in our driveway (all with the logo of that cute doggie with the scissors through its neck) and I surmised they invited irresponsible owners to abandon their charges. We frequently found an animal tied to the doorknob or wandering around the backyard.

The first family member to step out in the morning would shout back at the rest of us, "There's another dog tied to a van!"

Fudge!

Sometimes the animal became our household pet, and other times I'd badger friends to take it in. It was darn right hard for them to say, "No," once an abandoned pet had her four legs in the door and they had fed her a pork chop meant for dinner.

"Just keep her for a day," I'd coax, "and if it doesn't work out, I'll come by and pick her up. But, of course, her next stop will be the pound."

Worked every time!

I developed a reputation for pawning off orphan animals on friends and before too long, they wised up. When they spotted me ambling up the sidewalk with an unfamiliar pet, they hid behind their curtains and didn't answer the door.

During a summer break from college, Kris and I heard a dog whining in front of our house. The small, buff-colored cocker spaniel underneath our bushes wore a collar, so we hoped to return it to its owner. Kris edged behind the shrubs and attempted to secure it with a leash.

"Yeow, ouch!" she yelled. The ungrateful dog had bitten her. But she persevered, looped the leash around its neck and brought it into the house where it promptly peed.

We exhausted every lead to find its owner because, of course, the collar was just that—a collar with no tags, no ID, nothing to identify this temperamental little cocker. No doubt we should have paid more attention to his initial reaction to Kris' loving concern, but after that first bite, he returned Kris' love and selectively reserved his teeth for others. What could we do?

Kris named the dog Snookers, although Dr. Jekyll/Mr. Hyde would have been more appropriate. Schizophrenic Snookers could be friendly one second and snap at the hand in front of him the next. Our boys disliked and ignored him. Niel and I kept our distance as well. He was not a family pet—he was Kris' problem child.

A walk in the park one day almost ended in a lawsuit. A small child tried to pet him. Conveniently, the child's nose was right at Snooker's level and he just couldn't pass up the opportunity to take a hunk out of it—much wailing from the humans, none from Snookers.

When Kris went back to college after her summer break, Niel and I inherited Snookers. If we had company, Snookers would greet them by peeing. We learned to drag him into a bedroom beforehand, and he yowled the entire time. Except on Halloween, his howling hardly added to our home's ambience.

After Kris graduated from college, she again became Snooker's mistress, but by then Snookers was failing. The day arrived for his final visit to the vet, and she couldn't bring herself to take him.

Dave, our youngest, who was still at home and a frequent recipient of Snooker's bites, volunteered. Afterward, he said, "I only had a slight twinge of regret. That was one miserable dog."

But Dave was not immune to our family tradition of taking in stray orphans. After graduating from college and deciding he wanted nothing to do with his political science major, he spent hours in the basement huddled over his computer. I knew he was working on a novel. His remaining hours were divided between sleep and working in our office for his room and board. (I say "our" because by this time Niel had taken over my bookkeeping, payroll, van repair and slipped into the role of all-around housekeeper and cook as well.)

Several months into his project, Dave asked me for feedback, and after critiquing what he had written, together we decided he needed more life experience. He tapped his pencil on the desk to get my attention and said, "Say, Mom, what do you think about me being your apprentice?"

I was not surprised he had figured out that groomers earned four times that of office help. He spent several months at my side grooming, and I didn't even mind that he was receiving a free education after we had paid for four years of college. What really excited me was the possibility that he might eventually take over the business. He was a quick learner—a natural at working with dogs, and what was even better, he didn't mind grooming cats. How great was that?

Dave had been grooming for a few months when he encountered the pet groomer's occupational hazard. The day before Thanksgiving he was leaving his last client when he spotted a lanky black Labrador retriever loping down the sidewalk next to his van. The dog was dragging a clanking, bouncing chain behind him, and obviously had escaped from his home. He was having the time of his life. Dave had just put his elderly Lab, Ebony, to sleep and knew how heartbreaking it was to lose a pet. He left the van, captured the runaway and then, even though night was falling, drove around the neighborhood trying to locate the owner.

No luck.

He phoned the office "Mom, I got this Lab in the van with me that was roaming the streets and I can't find the owners. What should I do?"

"I guess you'll have to bring him home, but we have to find who he belongs to or get him to a shelter."

We called the Humane Society, the shelters and all the police stations in the precincts near where Dave had found him. Again we came up empty. I began to wonder if Dave was fated to own this dog, which was a twin to his deceased Ebony.

We had invited thirteen guests for Thanksgiving, and now we had a fourteenth—a strange, very large, rambunctious dog romping through the house. I called the "uninvited guest" Runner. On Thanksgiving Day, Runner assumed the role of host and, as only a Lab can do, enthusiastically welcomed each of our "invited guests" at the door by jumping on them and sealing his approval with a big lick. Oh, well, our friends were used to orphan dogs at our house. I was certain most were hoping we wouldn't have the gall to ask them to take Runner home with them.

Of course, all the shelters were closed until Monday. Four days later, when they reopened, we inquired whether they had room for a large dog. We learned that large dog crates were at a premium in shelters, and each facility advised us to call in a week. A week? Pointless! By then, Dave and Runner had bonded.

Runner was later renamed Jock, but he should have kept the original. That dog outraced and outlasted anyone chasing him and hurdled over six-foot-high obstacles like an Olympic champion. He escaped from our yard and home on a regular basis. His behavior explained the lack of response to the numerous "lost dog" notices we placed throughout Baltimore. It wasn't hard to guess that his previous owner probably had gotten fed up with playing posse and trying to track him down.

Dave wasn't disappointed that no one had claimed Jock. He said, "I guess he's mine now, Mom."

S'pose so.

One day, Jock slipped out the back door, cleared our extra-high fence and galloped down the street toward the Baltimore Beltway. As I chased him, he zigzagged through traffic on crowded streets. Cars screeched, horns honked and drivers yelled nasty words at both of us.

"Gotcha," I said as I cornered him in a yard, but he blew past me before I could grab his collar.

Jock raced through adjoining yards and jumped fences until he came to an abrupt stop at the chain link barrier bordering the beltway. He looked back to see me gaining on him and bounded along the fence until he wriggled through a hole he'd found. At that point, I was thoroughly disgusted with him and screamed, "Go ahead. Maybe it's your destiny to be killed by a car."

Mad as hell and out of breath, I trudged back to the house, enlisted Niel's help and returned to where Jock had slipped under the fence. I had calmed down and was just plain worried that I'd see a dead Jock by the edge of the road.

But, no. There he was, proudly sitting on *our* side of the fence and wagging his tail. Once the chase was over, he was no longer having fun. Tuckered out and ready to take a nap, he offered no resistance as we put him on a leash. Drooling and panting, he eagerly hopped into the car. Naughty dog!

When Dave bought his own home, Jock moved with him. Suddenly, it was way too quiet at our place. But we didn't rush to find another dog. Past experience told me an orphan was just around the corner. Actually, she was around several corners. In fact, she was about fifteen miles from our home.

I had an appointment to groom two dogs in Baltimore's Inner Harbor area. I had forgotten my grooming tools and radioed Niel to bring them to me. When I arrived at the client's home, the elderly husband asked if I could also clean up a small, caramel-colored cocker-poodle puppy. They had rescued it from two boys swinging her around in circles by her tail.

Of course, I could. How could anyone treat a puppy like that?

I found an old brush in the van and was in the middle of brushing the little one out when Niel arrived. He watched me work with the new pup and didn't seem in a hurry to leave.

He said, "She sure is cute, isn't she?"

"Sure is. The owners can't keep her—she's driving them and their older dogs crazy. I guess if they can't find a home for her, they'll have to take her to a shelter."

What had possessed me to utter the word "shelter?" That was our family's trigger word for "rescue that dog."

Scratching her behind her ears, he said, "Can't we take her? We have an 'opening' now, you know."

I did my best to nip it in the bud. "Opening? What opening? If I took in every stray dog, we'd be operating a kennel by now."

He sniffed, gave the pup one last pat, and left. I knew this conversation hadn't ended. When I came in that night, he mentioned the pup again.

Even though I was aware of the odds, I foolishly promised, "All right, if they still haven't found a home for her by Sunday evening, we'll go get her."

Two days later, we headed downtown to pick her up and all the way home, while I drove, she and Niel cuddled and nuzzled one another. Niel aptly named her Ginger, and although she loved us both, she was wild about Niel. She was happy each time we returned home, but if I came in first, she habitually peeked behind me to make sure the love of her life was also coming through that door.

Ginger was Miss Personality and the friendliest dog we owned. Unlike Snookers, everyone was her friend, and visitors couldn't help but succumb to her charm. She was with us for twelve years and unexpectedly died in the middle of the night. We buried her in our backyard and each time we passed the sliding doors, we gazed at her grave and teared up.

We wrapped her little pink collar around our desk lamp, and to this day, when glancing at it, remark, "Ginger, sweetie, we still miss you."

We lasted two weeks without our Ginger before Niel, moping around the house, said, "How about I search the Web and see if there's a site where they list dogs needing a home?"

An hour later he called, "Come here. I found this Petfinder.com link where they've got over 66,000 dogs. How about I look for a few in our area? We want a small female, right?"

"I guess. Where do they get all those dogs?"

"Let's see. It says they go to places where they know the dogs aren't kept more than a few days before they're put to sleep. They rescue them and send e-mails to everyone in the organization to see who has room for the dogs."

Niel hunched over his computer for several hours and handed me his research. "Here, I found twelve dogs that match our criteria. This little girl is in Pottstown, Pennsylvania. The woman has five dogs that they took out of a high-kill shelter in Tennessee. Wanna go up this weekend and check her out?"

The previously unwanted Sasha became a member of our family and still is today.

Pets added immeasurable love to my life. As far as grooming them, you would think that my own dogs would be ready to strut down the dog-show runway. That wasn't the case. Maybe it was because after I spent weeks in my van, my dog just became one dog too many—kind of like the cobbler's kids with holes in their shoes.

To this day, orphan dogs tug at my heart, but retired and living in a community where we're restricted to just owning Sasha, I can't take them in. Nonetheless, I feel sad when I see TV spots showing dogs and cats waiting for adoption. I'm tempted to run down and pick these homeless animals up. If left unhindered, I'd probably end up being the fabled "dog or cat lady." Every neighborhood has one.

I assume, since you're still reading, that you, too, care about dogs and cats. You probably view "The Animal Channel" and are appalled when a program features abused animals. You hate it when animal shelters are forced to euthanize pets because their cages are filled. Your heart goes out when you hear about a litter of kittens or pups being dropped off in a sack by the side of the road.

Here are several ways you can demonstrate your concern:

- Donate pet food, treats and toys to a shelter. Cash will go a long way, too
- Report animal cruelty when you discover it (and I don't care if it is your next-door neighbor).

- Have your own pets neutered or spayed.

- Purchase pets from a reputable breeder and not a "puppy mill." If you buy an animal from a pet shop, determine where they purchase their pets.

- But the very best way to show your love for animals is to adopt your next pet from a shelter. I guarantee that both you and your new friend will enrich each other's lives.

9
Unfulfilled Promises

Canine Clippers grew to running five vans full-time and soared to the top of the leader board as the largest mobile pet grooming firm in Maryland. But there was a dark lining to that silver cloud: It had been hard enough to find qualified groomers with just one van or two; now it became a major headache. My ad in *The Baltimore Sun* would run for weeks with nary an inquiry.

When someone with promise did show up, I discovered that the ones who loved animals didn't deal well with people, and that the people persons weren't all that talented working with animals. Finding the right combination in a groomer like Bonnie (despite her gypsy tendencies), was no small feat. I also realized there was a big difference between groomers who had a limited education and those who were second-career people.

The first category, groomers who barely made it out of grade school, much less high school, generally learned the trade by the seat of their pants. However, many didn't have people smarts. Such was the case with Fern.

Fern married and had children before she was sixteen. Little by little she educated herself by apprenticing to another groomer and practicing on her own show dogs. By the time she joined Canine Clippers, she was quite accomplished with many years of experience. But she had a gruff manner and repeatedly lost her temper when dealing with both dogs and clients.

Mrs. Silver phoned, "Jan, Fern's out there in the van grooming Sissy, and she's shouting at her. No one shouts at my Sissy."

"Thank you for telling me, Mrs. Silver. Fern's an excellent groomer and would never hurt Sissy, but sometimes she becomes a bit impatient. I'm going to phone her and ask what's going on."

"Don't bother. I'm going out to the van to tell her myself. And don't send Fern again."

While Fern was a great groomer, she frequently irritated clients. Shouting at the dogs was not her only downside. She also couldn't stifle her bad humor and had no clue how to pacify an owner. Every so often I would have a discussion with her about customer relations. She'd be fine for a few weeks and then I'd get another call.

But I didn't fire Fern. She was too good at her chosen profession.

Several secretaries I hired asked if I would train them to be groomers. After I spent months doing so, they would stay for a few weeks and then go work in a pet salon that wasn't quite so challenging. Finally, I wised up and refused to fall for that ruse.

When Margaret applied for our secretarial position, she was very upfront about her goals. She proposed, "I'll work as a secretary, but I'd really like to learn to groom. Could I work three days a week in the office and go along with you the other three days? I'll sign a contract that I'll work for you for one year."

I agreed and she kept her end of the bargain. She purchased a van and after the year was up, started a mobile pet grooming business of her own. We stayed friends.

The other category of groomers was people seeking a second or third career. Some were nurses, some teachers and some computer analysts.

Sandy was a hairdresser. During our interview she said, "I figured the dogs wouldn't talk back to me or complain about their hairdo."

What Sandy didn't take into account was that while the dogs wouldn't talk back, their owners would. I bet she was never bitten by a hairdressing client! She stayed with Canine Clippers for several years, but was overly picky about which dogs she would or would not groom, depending on their rotten temperament history. I didn't blame her—I felt the same way.

I found that although second-career people attended grooming school and were adequate groomers, most of them were used to dancing to their own tune and had difficulty taking direction. Grooming alone in a van was perfect for them. No one was looking over their shoulders and as far as I was concerned, if they pleased their customers, they pleased me.

By the time Eddie came along, I had considerable interviewing and hiring experience under my belt. However, that hardly qualified me as an expert.

Kris was home from college and overheard I was going to meet with someone called Eddie, "Mom, I wonder whether this might be the Eddie I worked with at Finished Dog?"

"What do you know about him?"

"Oh, Mom, they fired him because he was on drugs. Not only that, he was notorious for not showing up on Monday mornings."

I had major misgivings. Eddie's prompt arrival for the interview was a good sign, but his appearance—ugh. He looked like he had come from a day of pan-handling. His streaked jeans hung on a skin-and-bones frame. A large, unbuttoned and faded shirt with a pack of Marlboros peeking out of the pocket barely covered his equally oversized undershirt. Hard-toed hiking boots finished off his appearance on the bottom and Brylcreemed hair on top.

He picked at his grubby fingernails. His milky blue eyes never quite met mine. Even without Kris' warning, I knew right away something was seriously wrong. I was confident I had pegged this one.

Scanning his application, I concentrated on the "previous employment" section. Yep, Eddie had worked for Finished Dog and was, indeed, "that Eddie."

I sat back, folded my arms and said, "Eddie, I believe you worked with my daughter, Kris, when you were at Finished Dog." There was no point mincing words. "Also, there's a rumor you're doing drugs."

Eddie didn't answer. I waited, but speechless Eddie had ceased fidgeting and appeared shell-shocked. Unimpressed with this squirrelly guy, I decided to make short shrift of the interview. Eddie obviously was not Canine Clippers' employee material. But then he piped up, "Yes, Miz Nieman, I've had a bit of trouble with drugs. But I've just been released from rehab, and I'm asking for a chance to get my life back."

I had expected a denial. It was my turn to be flustered, "Aaahh," I stalled, "could I have some proof of that, Eddie?"

"Yes, ma'am. You could contact my drug program counselor."

After years of sitting in church pews absorbing sermons stressing mercy and compassion, it seemed God was challenging me to act. The business side of me warned, "You're asking for trouble. You know what the outcome of this is going to be." The spiritual side admonished, "What about that scripture commanding us to feed and cloth others in need? Doesn't that apply to employees, too? This is your chance to practice what you've learned."

I argued with God, "But Lord, this is business with a capital 'B.' Surely you don't expect me to hire this guy who is guaranteed not to work out."

No thundering voice delivered advice from heaven, no printing on Eddie's shirt advertised, "Hire Me," no on-the-spot guidance either way. This would take some mulling over and prayer. I thanked Eddie and said I'd get back to him.

With no further applicants knocking down my door for the grooming position, I phoned Eddie's drug counselor and he confirmed that Eddie was attending sessions and "coming along."

Just in case Eddie wasn't "coming along" as quickly as I hoped, I wanted to give myself an out. So I told Eddie up front, "I'll give you a try, but I'm keeping the ad in the paper. If I see any evidence of drug use, you won't be working for Canine Clippers." I added, "By the way, you've got to dress more professionally."

To my surprise, on the first day of work Eddie arrived a half hour early wearing a slick, new grooming smock over clean jeans. I kept my astonishment to myself. Since Eddie required no training, he jumped into a van, familiarized himself with the setup, mapped out his route and drove off.

Throughout the week his customers phoned. "My dog has never looked so cute. Please note on Mimi's record that I want only Eddie to groom her." Eddie was one heck of a groomer!

Was this God's answer? Was I being rewarded for taking a chance? I took it as a sign and stopped the ad.

On a Monday, a month later, Eddie phoned in. "Miz Nieman, I've got a terrific migraine and won't be in today. Could you please add my dogs to the end of each day this week? I'll work overtime to groom all of them."

My radar was activated immediately. "Well," I said to Niel, "at least he's taking responsibility for the doggies assigned to him." Although he kept his word and worked late the rest of the week, I remained alert for future signs of trouble.

Two weeks later at 5:30 on another Monday morning, his live-in girlfriend called. "Eddie's grandmother just passed away. He told me to tell you he won't be in until later in the week. Please reschedule his appointments for next weekend."

He groomed a few of his missed dogs, but I had to go out evenings and pick up the rest of them. I so wanted Eddie to work out, but it wasn't the first "dead grandmother" excuse I'd heard.

Eddie phoned in several weeks later, again on a Monday. "Miz Nieman, I had some wisdom teeth removed and got an infection. They want me to go to the hospital."

When Eddie returned, he had difficulty looking directly at me, but he assured me his problems were over. Unconvinced, I wondered what new lesson the Lord had in mind for me.

I bargained, "Here's the deal Lord, I'll give Eddie one more chance. If he or his girlfriend phone in once more with some lame excuse, that's it."

The next Monday morning, my caller ID warned that Eddie was on the line. I was tempted to let the voicemail take the call. On the other hand, the time had come to terminate Eddie's employment. Enough, already!

I picked up the phone and Eddie's girlfriend sobbed, "Eddie won't be in to work today. He overdosed and died last night"

I was stunned, but before I could offer condolences, she gulped, "Would you please send Eddie's last check to me? He's got bills to pay."

Half an hour later Eddie's mother phoned. "Does Eddie have another check coming? If he does, that should come to me. I'm his only living relative. Don't you send it to that woman he lives with."

On advice from our attorney, we sent Eddie's paycheck to his estate at his home address. I suspected Eddie was not "estate material," but we followed orders. If either his girlfriend or mother forged his signature it was the bank's problem. The check was never cashed.

Although I was forewarned about Eddie's drug problem, I had hired him anyway. I could hardly believe my good fortune at signing up someone familiar with van grooming and had chosen to ignore red light alerts. On the one hand, I was furious that he conned me into believing he had overcome his addiction; on the other, his death shocked and saddened me. What was even more troubling was that his girlfriend and mother were battling over his last week's wages without seemingly caring about him.

I told God, "I'm a bit disappointed you didn't come through on this one." No answer—again.

Willie's story was both similar and different. He showed up for the interview wearing a professional white hospital jacket that looked dressy next to his chocolate skin. He was well groomed—clean fingernails, spotless white Nikes and creased jeans. I was impressed with the contrast to Eddie.

"And where did you get your training?" I asked Willie.

He opened his flat, well worn wallet and pulled out a tightly folded paper. Carefully opening it, he presented it with pride. It said, "Master Groomer, Graduate of California Grooming School."

"So, you graduated from a pet grooming school in California?"

"Yes'm."

"And how long have you been working as a pet groomer?"

"Oh, say 'bout twenty years."

"Any references?"

"Well, ma'am, I does in California, but I jus' arrive here in Balmer."

While Willie's grooming certificate read "Master Groomer," he wasn't the most promising applicant, mainly because of his poor English. But, I was already into the third week of running that groomer ad. "Well, Willie, can you spend tomorrow with me in the van so I can observe your technique and how you handle dogs?"

Willie hesitated and said, "Ma'am, I hitched a ride today but I gotta catch a bus to get here. You on a bus line?"

Why hadn't Willie thought of this before traveling to my office? Did Willie even drive, much less possess a license? And if he actually did, how many points had he accumulated?

As if he read my thoughts, Willie again reached for his wallet and produced a Maryland driver's license. Yep, there was Willie's photo.

"How come you have a Maryland license, when you said you recently moved here?"

"Ma'am, I lived here for years but wanted to give California a try—didn't work out, so I moved back."

I wondered if I was hiring another vagabond who would set up housekeeping in my van. A fleeting thought of possibly renting out vans as housing units rattled around in my brain before I dismissed it. I was a grooming business owner, not a landlord.

The next day Willie and I drove off to check out his grooming, driving and people skills. Willie knew how to handle difficult dogs, and all of them looked sharp and stylish when he returned them to their owners. He drove the van around town with ease and took a few shortcuts unknown to me. Clients were charmed by his manners and his obvious love for their pets. Had I really hit the jackpot this time?

It was decision time. I didn't want to don my grooming smock and jump in a van to hit the road full-time again while I continued searching for someone else to do that. But unless I hired a standby employee for when someone was sick or left, I was the designated emergency groomer. Despite my concern I was taking on another Gypsy, I took a chance on Willie.

During the next several weeks, I followed up on Willie. I phoned his customers, and without exception they loved both his work and his attitude. I started to relax and congratulated myself on hiring a winner.

Payday arrived and Willie asked, "Could you cash this for me? I don't got no bank account yet."

We cashed Willie's paychecks for the next several weeks. We presumed that eventually Willie would find housing, buy a car and open a checking account.

A month later, a client phoned, "I have a West Highland terrier, and he doesn't look like he usually does after his grooming. Does your groomer know what a Westie is supposed to look like?"

"Can you explain what's different this time?"

"His head doesn't look right. He has tufts around his ears and long eyebrows."

She was right. Her description didn't match how a Westie should be groomed. When Willie arrived that afternoon, I told him about the complaint. His eyes focused on the ceiling. Seeming to search his memory as to which dog we were discussing, he finally said, "That's a Westie? I thought it was a white Scottie!"

I was floored. Westies were white, Scotties were black. How could he possibly confuse the two breeds? How much communicating did he do with the client? I returned the client's money. Willie acted chagrined and I thought, "Well, everyone is entitled to one strike."

Strike Two phoned the following day. "I think your groomer has been drinking. I smelled alcohol on him. Don't ever send him back!"

Did I have an employee who was drinking and driving, not to mention grooming dogs with sharp tools? I was ready to stand behind my groomer, but Willie and I were going to have a serious discussion.

When Willie returned that afternoon, I immediately confronted him. "Were you drinking today, Willie? One of your clients said she smelled alcohol on your breath."

"No, ma'am! You can't drink an' groom dogs. They know it every time. She musta smelled some pills I gotta take."

I warned him that he could not drink on the job and continue to work for me, but he appeared crestfallen at my accusation. Feeling guilty and wanting to believe him, I offered to drive him home.

As I headed into Baltimore, Willie, who normally talked non-stop, was mum. He fidgeted with his sleeves and couldn't seem to control his jittery leg. When I asked him what street he lived on, he advised me to turn here, turn there.

We stopped at one house and he reconsidered. "No, think I'll stay with someone else tonight." He gave me directions to another house a few blocks away, where he jumped out and waved me off.

I concluded he lived on the streets.

Willie was a tad late for work the next day—an ominous sign. I tried to edge closer to him to catch a whiff as he passed by me, but cagy Willie was moving too fast. Grabbing his routing sheet and client records, he was out the door, into his van, and down the road before I could inhale.

At 2:00 Strike Three phoned. "Your groomer's been drinking. I'm blind and can't hear worth a damn, but ain't nothing wrong with my sniffer. That man was snookered. He reeked. I didn't let him touch my dog, and I'll never use your services again."

I got on the two-way radio and told him to come in.

A few minutes later, the radio crackled. "Miz Nieman, this Willie. I jus' been in a accident."

"Are you OK, Willie? Is anyone hurt?"

"No ma'am. I'm OK, but the van pretty busted up. But I got me a witness. It wasn't my fault."

Amazed, I said, "You have a witness of the accident?"

"He be riding with me, my friend."

Willie knew the rules: No one but the groomer should be in the van.

Niel and I were tense and furious as we drove to the accident scene. When we arrived, we found the van drivable and no one injured. Predictably, the witness/passenger buddy had disappeared. Willie claimed the other driver jumped the green light. That party insisted Willie had run a red light. Our hunch was the other driver had a leg up on the truth.

Grateful that he hadn't been subjected to a breathalyzer test (which he would have failed), I gave him an aspirin for his supposed headache, and fired him.

Little did I know my relationship with Willie wasn't even close to being terminated. A week later we received a notice from Workers' Compensation. Willie had filed a disability claim.

What nerve! We suspected Willie's headache had been caused by something other than the accident and decided to contest his allegation. We arrived at court full of self-righteous indignation. Willie was nowhere to be seen.

Our case was called, and we approached the bench. The judge shuffled some papers and peered at us through eyeglasses slipping down the bridge of his nose. "This case has been dismissed," he announced. "The plaintiff has been extradited back to California for parole violation."

I said to Niel, "Extradited? Like back to jail?"

Returning home, I rifled through his employee folder searching for the copy of his "grooming certificate." When I plucked it from the file, I found, no longer surprised, that it had been bestowed on him while attending the State of California's pet grooming "in house" rehabilitation program. Willie had been trained as a groomer while serving jail time.

Willie looked very good on the surface, but if I had examined his "diploma" more closely, I probably wouldn't have hired him. At the very least, when the first complaint came in, I should have paid more attention. However, Willie was, for four weeks, indeed a Master Groomer.

"You know," Niel said about Eddie and Willie after they were both gone, "you might have done better just picking someone off the street."

"I think I did," I said back.

It was a real shame. They both brought such talent, wonderful personalities, and an understanding of customer relations to their profession. If it hadn't been for their addictions to drugs and alcohol, they would have been perfect employees, not unfulfilled promises.

10
Merrily We Roll Along

Merrily we roll along, roll along, roll along...or not. In time I learned to cope with employee headaches, and they rolled off my back. But as I became more and more absorbed with keeping the vans rolling, I developed a love/hate relationship with them. When their systems worked well, I loved owning Canine Clippers, but as time went on, that proved to be the exception. At least once a week, one of the five vans was sitting at Freddy's Campers or taking up space in Mike's garage while we waited for a part to come in, and I grew to hate them.

"Just one week, just one week," I complained to Niel, "it would be nice to have them all on the road." But that was seldom the case, and in the end, it wasn't the clients, the dogs or the employees that frustrated me the most, it was those grooming vans.

When I walked from van to van every morning, turning the key in each ignition, one or more decided it was their morning to catch forty winks. They were not budging out of that driveway.

Niel and I found humor in the clients, the groomers and the pets. After several years of horrendous repair bills, we found nothing amusing about the vans.

The first major glitch resulted from Lenny, the van conversion guy, disregarding my directions on Van Number One. He and I had argued for days over the location of the holding tank into which the dirty water flowed.

Lenny advised, "Jan, that holding tank should be bolted in back under the van."

"I don't think so, Lenny. The water in there will turn to ice if the temperature drops below 32 degrees. It should be inside the van, where I can place heaters next to it so it doesn't freeze."

"Nah, it doesn't get that cold underneath a van."

"Well, I don't want to chance it and want it inside."

Assuming I had made my point, I realized Lenny had prevailed only when I picked up the van. There, under the van's rear, hung the two-by-four-foot black steel beauty.

I would discover, come winter, Lenny had been unable to reverse the laws of physics, and by day's end, the tank held a frozen block of filthy water.

Annoyed, I canceled the following week's appointments while the tank thawed out in the warmth of Lenny's shop. He was peevish as he removed the tank and reconfigured the space to accommodate it inside the van. When finished he generously offered, "I won't charge you folks extra for that."

I considered sarcastically thanking him for my one-week unpaid vacation, but thought better of it. I might need his services to fix another problem caused by him.

That solved one snag, but as temperatures dropped, I discovered another. If night temperatures dipped below 15 degrees, come morning, no matter how many small electrical heaters I propped close to the water lines, ice would be blocking a line—somewhere.

All of the water systems were in the rear, and I first had to get the back open—if I could. Frequently, liquid had pooled on the floor and the rear doors were frozen to the body of the van. All the pulling and tugging in the world wasn't going to dislodge them.

In the pitch black, early morning hours, with the wind whipping around the van and up my fanny, I clutched the flashlight with one hand and aimed a hair dryer at the bottom sill until the doors thawed enough to be yanked open. Then, and only then, was I able to pinch the plastic water lines, find the ice and point the dryer at them until water flowed again.

What a thrill when we graduated to multiple vans with the resulting multiple blockages. When that happened, I flung open the house door with more force than necessary, stomped down the hallway and shouted, "Niel! I need help out here!"

My spouse would groggily pull on his pants and pour a cup of coffee, seemingly oblivious to the urgency of the situation. The clock would tick closer to that first 8:00 a.m. appointment as we frantically raced from van to van. Our groomers would soon arrive expecting their mobile pet salons to be cozy and warm *with* running water.

If you wondered why I didn't simply park them in a heated garage overnight, you may not be intimately acquainted with the phrase "profit margin." If I paid garage rent, rather than parking five vans in my convenient and *free* driveway, I added another expense to an already hemorrhaging budget. I may not have thought of every obstacle when I launched Canine Clippers Mobile Pet Grooming, Inc., but I did know there was no garage in my vans' futures.

Another thing I had not thought of when I had considered the van ready to go was that running both the hair dryer and the air conditioning unit would overload the ancient electrical systems in many of Baltimore's one-hundred-year-old homes. Mrs. O'Brien lived in one of those, and she and her home were about the same age. She shared her home with Puddles, a Yorkshire terrier that matched Mrs. O'Brien's longevity in dog years. But her pup was still spritely, adorable and a dream to work with.

I was in groomer heaven, with a great dog in a cool van on a hot day. Puddles had been clipped and bathed, and was ready for drying, but as I switched on the hair dryer, the electric went off. Unable to leave Puddles in the van, I wrapped a towel around him and trotted back to Mrs. O'Brien's home.

Puddles was thrilled. I was not.

Mrs. O'Brien had no clue where her breaker or fuse box was located. She pointed to the basement door. The entire house had lost power, and I groped in darkness for the stairs.

I said, "Mrs. O'Brien, stay upstairs. I don't want you to fall." If it was my lucky day, I might serendipitously come across the breaker box, throw the switch, jog back up the stairs and speed back to the van with a disappointed Puddles. However, fate would not be smiling on me that day, and I discovered that her electrical box held fuses. The final straw was that Mrs. O'Brien had no idea where her replacements were located. On the other hand, I made up some time since I didn't have to dry Puddles.

As my experience with tricky power outages multiplied, I became somewhat gun-shy. I tried drying doggie without the A/C running. Within minutes both of us were close to a heat stroke, but without an alternative, I usually left them to air dry and charged the client less. Yep, summer grooming was almost as bad as dealing with the ice in winter. Spring and fall were lovely, though, thank you very much.

I had dreamed up additional plans for the interior of that experimental first van and had told Niel, "Wouldn't it be nifty to install a small propane stove to heat water for a cup of tea now and then?"

My fantasy grew to the possibility of throwing in an air mattress for camping trips. After all, the van had water, a water heater, a furnace and now a small stove. Why not?

Here's why not. After one week, I knew I wasn't going to heat anything on that stove. Dog hair was everywhere. I breathed it; I drank it; I snorted it. I had visions of a surgeon pulling hair balls out of my lungs and wondering if I had been raised by wolves.

Unbeknownst to me, fuzzy clumps attached themselves to my rear making me a groomer Playboy Bunny look-alike. Itchy hair snaked into my bra, and when I undressed at night, I discovered the stuff had filtered to other unmentionable places. Nope, dog hair brought the idea of camping in a van to a screeching halt.

Remember Mike, my repair man? He admonished me, "Mrs. Nieman, you gotta keep that dog hair from getting under the hood. I want to show you something." With a sadistic gleam in his eye, he continued, "This is what I pulled out from underneath your dash."

He reached into a Hefty bag and pulled out what looked like a small cocker spaniel, or at least the pelt of one.

"And just how would I do that?" I griped. "I'm lucky if I can get the groomers to vacuum the dog hair off the floor."

Well aware that his future income depended on plucking pet hair from other van nooks and crannies, Mike tut-tutted, and smirked. He knew there was no solution to the gathering woolies and there was gold in "them there hairs."

Dog hair, clinging to shoes and clothing, filtered into the house. Like tumbleweed it drifted down hallways and collected in the living room and bedrooms.

Riding to church on Sunday mornings, Niel and I, monkey-like, plucked dog hair off each other's clothes. We were embarrassed when helpful church members sitting behind us discreetly removed additional strays. Had we known that we'd go through boxes of adhesive hair removal products, we would have invested in those companies.

With the passage of time, Niel viewed the elderly vans less as a body repair project and more as an antique vehicle restoration. He learned to solder metal panels to the rusted doors when Extend (a rust neutralizer), Bondo body filler, aluminum tape, and spray paint no longer did the job.

Water heater covers, sliding van doors, exhaust pipes or any part attached to the outside of the van frame with bolts eventually worked themselves loose and landed on the road.

One morning, Ted, a relatively new employee, called in on the radio. "Jan, I'm stuck in the middle of Liberty Road and Milford Mill. I think something fell off underneath the van."

Niel raced to the busy intersection. It was spectacular how one drive shaft in the middle of the street could foul up traffic. The van was empty, no driver to be found.

I mailed Ted his paycheck.

Many mornings when I crawled out of my cozy bed to start up the five vans, I was greeted by a malfunctioning brake, directional signal or taillight.

Niel joked, "Did you notice that when you see a car with a non-working brake light, it's generally the same make as our vans?"

Another business we supported, and likely would've folded without us, was Phil and Norm's Towing. We phoned them so often that our conversations had a familiar exchange.

"Hello. Phil and Norm's Towing."

"Hi, this is Canine Clippers. We have a van down."

"OK, give me the address and we'll tow it down to Mike's."

"Right, we'll pick up the groomer; you know where the keys are."

"Is it 'old blue' or one of the others?"

We broke down in ritzy areas, in scary neighborhoods, and on the beltway at its entrance and exit ramps. Some mornings when a van refused to start, Phil and Norm even towed us from our own driveway. We were on a first name basis with all their drivers. The company billed us monthly and could have billed us weekly. Mike was never surprised when one of our vans, which had broken down over the weekend and was towed to his garage, greeted him on a Monday morning.

Why, you ask, didn't we replace those old vans with new ones? Ready for this? A new grooming van cost about $62,000. One dog grooming averaged fifty dollars (and groomers that worked for me received half of that). Even if I worked six days a week, fifty-two weeks a year (and don't forget interest, insurance, taxes and repairs) I would be an octogenarian before even one van was paid off!

Since it wasn't feasible to invest enormous sums of money into a business when we were nearing retirement, we found ourselves caught in an ongoing struggle to keep the aging fleet running. Toward the end, we relegated one van to standby mode, ready to race to where another was disabled.

If my business hadn't depended on those vans, it would have been enormously successful. After all, there were plenty of dirty dogs, mostly wonderful customers and skilled employees out there. But our downfall wasn't limited to the vans' operation. Grooming equipment inside also added to our grief and most of it involved water.

Water, you say? Oh, yeah. Water was everywhere, except where or when it was needed. I became obsessed with water problems. A van without running hot and cold water wasn't a grooming van at all. It was just a cubicle with loads of pricey equipment.

Every week brought yet another water crisis. The pump stopped pumping and the heater didn't heat. A holding tank filled with fifty gallons of water developed cracks that even gobs of Crazy Glue could no longer seal. A drain clogged, tubing sprung leaks, and on and on, ad nauseam. The continued water malfunctions so disturbed me that my nightmares were not about crazy clients, vicious dogs or horrible employees. No, they were about those vans.

One time the Environmental Protection Agency sited us for dripping water from a van as we merrily traveled along. Some groomer hadn't closed the dump valve. I found out about it when a letter from the EPA arrived calling my attention to the problem; I panicked and yelped, "But it's just water! It's not any different from washing a car in a driveway!"

The EPA didn't see it that way and threatened us with a $500 fine and a warning that they had the power to close us down. After that, I became the Canine Clippers Resident Nag about those open dump covers.

One of the first questions a prospective client asked was, "Do you use the water over again?"

Yuk! Used water was *dirty* because dead fleas, bugs, filthy hair, or worst of all, a turd or two were floating in it. To bathe the next dog in that stuff would have been disgusting and unhealthy for both dog and groomer. The Center for Disease Control might have taken an interest in our questionable hygienic practices.

I sighed and launched into a description of how the water systems operated. "There are two large holding tanks under the bathing tub. One holds fresh water and the other one is empty until you bathe a dog. Then that dirty water drains into the empty tank."

That usually satisfied female inquirers. Males wanted more details. They loved checking out the van's innards and hearing how everything worked. Guys were impressed with my knowledge of the water systems. I wished some of our groomers had been similarly interested.

Pam, a second-career gal, sounded panicky as she shouted into the cell phone (we had finally joined the rest of the world and dumped the radios). "Jan, the tub won't drain! What should I do?"

"Is there anything clogging the strainer?"

"There is no strainer. I took it out because the tub drains too slowly with it in."

Thank you, Pam. After Niel disassembled the drain hose and removed wads of dog hair, he told Pam, "Leave the strainer in the tub."

But Pam didn't have the patience to wait. She wanted that water out of the tub—fast. She also didn't believe Niel and thought she could get away with removing the strainer. A few weeks later, Pam once again had a clogged drain hose.

That evening when she complained, Niel said, "Pam, how about you and I unplug it together. I'll let you remove the hair deposits yourself. That way, when it stops up again, you'll know how to do it."

There was some pretty gross stuff in that drain, and after that learning experience, Pam kept the strainer in place.

Fred, a prospective customer, was satisfied we wouldn't be bathing his cherished pet in dirty water, but that triggered another question. "So what do you do with the water at the end of the day?"

I elaborated. "The groomer attaches a hose, turns on a pump, and the dirty water is pumped into the sewer."

"Well, that's quite a system, isn't it?"

"You have no idea," I said, wanting to add, "when the finicky thing actually works."

In theory, dumping was simple. Water was pumped out through the drain hose and into the basement toilet. But, a problem arose when Van Number Three rolled in and parked behind Number One and Number Two. Because the driveway sloped toward the street, no matter how many pumps we used, they weren't powerful enough to suck out the water from any van parked behind Number Two. As a result, our one-lane driveway forced us to play musical vans every night, shifting each van in and out of the driveway until all were drained.

I became an expert at recognizing dripping fluids by color: green meant coolant; brown meant engine; red meant transmission or power steering. Clear liquids required closer examination. Was it the radiator, a water line or a water pump? In winter, icicles extending from the bottom of the van to the driveway pinpointed the break—very pretty, but sinister—something major inside had sprung a water leak!

Freddy of Freddy's Campers was our "go to" guy when those systems inside the van broke down. It invariably cost a minimum of $500 (the usual round number) to fix and a week off the road waiting for the part to arrive. Neither the groomers nor I could afford the loss. Frequently, it was the end of the road for them with us, and they moved on to a stationary pet grooming salon. Me? No choice. After a van came in, I worked late into the night grooming the rescheduled animals until the van was back on the road. If the groomer who was supposed to be in the van hadn't taken flight and quit, I gave him or her my earnings.

Bursting water lines and hoses drove us crazy. They seemed to have a mind of their own and frequently broke away from a fitting, dumping fifty gallons of water. It was particularly exciting if a line broke while a groomer was driving and water sloshed back and forth inside the van like a wave at Disney's Surf Pool.

Going to the Dogs

Employees were frantic when they called into the office, "There's water running all over the floor of the van! I can't stop it. What do I do?"

"Did you shut off the water pump?"

"I don't think so!"

"Well, turn it off and come in. We'll see if we can fix it."

Or, "Turn it off and Niel will head out to where you are. Clip the dog first. By then he should arrive to fix the break."

Water pumps! Ah, water pumps. Each van was equipped with one of these miserable, undependable gizmos. They were finicky contraptions, and if a ground wire corroded, they decided it was time to stop pumping, usually when a soaped-up dog was in the tub. Each groomer stashed several jugs of water in the wheel wells to finish rinsing an animal, should the unthinkable happen. But when the unthinkable happened in winter, the water in those jugs was frozen. Besides, in the case of a large, hairy dog, two gallons of water didn't come close to rinsing out all the suds.

Carrying a fifty-pound, totally lathered up Spike and standing at her door, I said, "Excuse me, Mrs. Dodd, I think my water pump gave out. Would it be possible for me to rinse off Spike in your laundry tub?"

What could Mrs. Dodd say, other than, "Yes"?

I didn't think Mrs. Dodd was too fond of the dog hair all over her basement after I dried Spike. The idea was to keep the mess in my van, not her home. Not only had that little water pump fouled up my day, it didn't bode well for a tip either. In fact, I was lucky that she paid me.

Rather than running to Freddy's Campers each time a water pump failed, we purchased five at a time and stocked them in our basement. Niel became quite adept at detaching the broken pump from a water line and installing a new one without losing a drop from the fifty gallon water tank.

Not only did water woes aggravate my groomers and me, but they upset our customers, too. Mrs. Winkler was beyond angry when she shouted into the phone. "Your groomer dumped brown water all over our new driveway and it won't wash off!"

I knew exactly where she lived and all the houses were, indeed, spanking new with pristine asphalt driveways. But how could we have left a brown stain? There was nothing in that water except shampoo. I promised her I would come out and take a look.

Sure enough, there was a large, rusty-looking, blotch, but I couldn't fathom how our van could have been the offender. Surely it came from some other service company's truck.

Mrs. Winkler wasn't buying it. She spouted, "It wasn't there before you guys came and it was there after you left!"

I saw her point.

We filed a claim with our insurance company. The agent took a gander at the stain, and he, too, could not figure out how it had happened. He said his company most likely would deny the claim because the owner could not prove it was Canine Clipper's van that discolored the driveway.

I loved being caught in the middle of a "Not Us" argument. I didn't want to pay for a driveway cleaning, but I also knew that bad news traveled fast. The upshot—I scoured the driveway on hands and knees with every cleaning agent from Home Depot, while Mrs. Winkler, spying through her custom-made walnut shutters, monitored my lack of progress.

An hour later I hadn't made any headway. My legs ached and my knees were scraped. Caustic solvents blistered my hands and I wondered, yet again, how I got myself into these predicaments. I limped to her door, and angry at myself that I had tried to clean her driveway on the cheap, I apologized. "I'm sorry. I was unable to remove the brown spot. I'm going to have to call a professional driveway cleaner." I never found out from either the cleaning firm or Mrs. Winkler whether the spot was removed.

Originally, I thought our old vans were the only ones that dripped, seeped and gushed. But after I was in business for about ten years and more groomers were becoming mobile, we compared notes. Sure enough, they all leaked and I discovered water, water everywhere was simply another occupational hazard.

11

Pit Stops

. . . .

The morning was typical—scheduling a dog to fill a cancellation, moving the vans out of the driveway and getting myself out of the house. My son, Dave, was still new to the job, and on that fall day I was tickled to be on the road with him. Dave slid into the driver's seat and we headed to the other side of town for our first appointment.

I planted my coffee mug into its holder and relaxed. It seemed like an opportune moment, since he was quickly picking up grooming skills, to tell him about some of the unexpected challenges of his new career.

"Dave, there are disadvantages to every occupation. You'll discover that the drawback for a mobile groomer is spending the whole day in a van from sunup to sundown and locating a restroom from time to time."

"Mom," he said, "I don't think I need training on where to find a bathroom."

"Trust me, Dave, what I'm about to tell you may become your number one priority."

He sighed. "Talk away. I'm listening."

"You're going to be on a tight time schedule and when nature calls, you'll want to be familiar with the closest pit stop. It's to your advantage to note where fast food places are located."

I considered that Dave, being a guy, maybe didn't share my standards, but I plowed ahead anyway and for the rest of our day told him how I ranked potty facilities.

Topping my list were major fast food chains, because with few exceptions, they cleaned and stocked their restrooms daily. As I drove from home to home, I learned to tuck their locations in the back of my mind. I could tell you the distance to the nearest McDonald's, Wendy's or Taco Bell from any Baltimore intersection.

My personal favorite was Burger King, where I could sneak past the customers waiting in line and shimmy down that side hall to the restroom. The employees were a happy bunch—joking with one another and taking no notice of me as I bypassed their buck-fifty drinks. I appreciated that I could wedge my quart-sized water container under their accommodating high faucets in the restroom and save a bundle.

The one drawback to Burger King was that, if I actually intended to purchase lunch, their single line for customers didn't generally move fast enough for a time-crunched driver. Ideally, it would have been wonderful to sit down, relax and eat inside. But if I lucked out and the queue wasn't winding back and forth through the ropes, I'd at least order something to eat in the van while I traveled to the next client.

Dave did quite well with his clipper work, scissoring and trimming nails. With both of us working on the dogs, we were ahead of schedule and stopped for lunch at my top-ranked fast food emporium.

I ordered a cheeseburger and declined the offer of drinks, grinning conspiratorially at Dave while hiding my water container behind me.

Dave grinned back, and not needing to watch his calories like his mother, ordered three cheeseburgers without fixins. Over lunch I resumed sharing my pit stop experiences.

Convenience stores ranked second on my list. They were, well, convenient, but the owners turned sullen when I asked, "Sir, do you mind if I use your restroom?"

I guessed the answer to that was "yes," when frowning they nodded me to the rear and occasionally chastised me grumbling, "Ma'am, our restrooms aren't for the general public."

If I was in a rotten mood I retorted, "If you sell prepared food, the law says you must supply a restroom."

Most likely, I was on shaky ground questioning that "prepared food" part. It appeared the only time hands touched food was when they rammed a wiener onto the spit. But usually I didn't have time to quibble as I dashed to the back.

These places chose to play hide-and-seek with their unidentified restrooms, and I frequently found myself opening the storeroom door before locating the real McCoy. Unlike fast food places, most convenience store restrooms were unisex. Think toilet seats left in the "up" position. While sidling past mops, pails and stacks of paper goods, I noted the toilet paper location and grabbed a roll—just in case—and did not waste quality time perusing the reading material scratched on the walls.

However, besides cheap soft drinks (not the bottled ones—I go for the help-yourself fountain variety), there was one advantage to convenience store pit stops. As I sat there, I could jot down on their industrial strength toilet paper a few items to complete my supper and pick them up on my way out.

Those purchases qualified me as a bona fide paying customer and usually earned me a smile and a "Thank you. Come in again."

Not if I could help it.

After our quick lunch we hopped in the van, and Dave drove to our fourth appointment while I chatted about gas station pit stops. With their questionable standards of cleanliness, they rated near the bottom, but there were occasions when I had no choice. If I had a full gas tank, I hoped the inside attendant wouldn't notice that my van wasn't parked at a pump gulping petrol.

In one particular instance, I assumed my nonchalant expression as I sauntered in. "Wonder if I could use your restroom?"

When the attendant answered, "Sure, sweet thing," without looking up from his *Playboy*, I knew he hadn't noticed my soaking wet smock covered with dog hair, fuzz hanging off my jeans-clad butt, and the fact that I was old enough to be his mother.

"You'll need a key, though."

"Mmmm, where would I find it?"

Still absorbed in his magazine, he thumbed toward the rear garage, "Just go into the bay there and ask Kenny."

Kenny chewed on a toothpick and nodded his head in the direction of a key on a hook wedged between the Goodyear tire display and "Drink Hires Root Beer" sign. While I stepped over scattered tools and parts, he and the other guys paused, not bothering to conceal their inspection of the female invading their territory.

I checked the supply of bathroom tissue before I closed the door, only to discover the lock didn't work. Unpleasant odors permeated the concrete stall, and so I took shallow breaths. I peed quietly—which is tricky after waiting until the last minute—and regretted my previous half-gallon thirst quencher. Horrified, I heard footsteps clomping towards the restroom. Before I could yell, "Occupied!" the door swung open and...I hated service station pit stops!

Dave and I worked together on our fourth dog of the day, a Lhasa apso. I was grateful to have him along as that little guy, like most Lhasas, insisted on hugging the table during his entire grooming. While one of us kept a hand under his tummy to hold him up, the other clipped him. By the time we were finished, we were both exhausted and didn't have the energy to talk while riding to our next appointment.

Our fifth dog was a Lab which needed only a bath and nail trim, and Dave groomed the dog by himself. I chilled out and read my *Groomer to Groomer* magazine.

After I finished an article about "Ear Infections–More Than Just Dirty Ears," I felt relaxed enough to share my past experiences with client bathrooms.

I told Dave since I was providing a service to dog owners who had the means to pay for our pricey coming-to-your-home rates, I had thought that using their facilities would be the best solution, rather than hunting for alternatives. Not so. Pet owner bathrooms could be "chancy."

If I was lucky enough to arrive at a regular client's home when nature called, I'd usually hit the jackpot. Most, but not all, beat public facilities.

"Hi, Mrs. Ramstead. Nice to see you again. Do you mind if I use your bathroom before I begin grooming Dinky?"

This request seemed to work well, especially since Mrs. Ramstead appreciated her pet being handled by a "focused" professional. However, if Mr. Ramstead answered the door, I was bashful about asking a man whether I could use his bathroom, and stalled my discomfort until I reached my next appointment.

"But, Dave," I said, "being a guy, that wouldn't be a drawback for you. On the other hand you might be more reticent about asking a female client."

I went on. "Emergency pit stops at a *new* customer's home are inadvisable. No matter how grand the house appears, if the owner's unprepared for guests, the bathroom could be in a similar condition."

"What do you mean, Mom?"

"No towels, no soap, no bathroom tissue."

I laughed as I told Dave about one case when I had asked to use a customer's bathroom.

The Smiths were a lovely couple, and I had groomed their little Pepper, a mixed-breed dog, for several years. Mr. Smith was having a difficult recovery from recent hernia surgery.

When I asked Mrs. Smith if I could use her bathroom, she hesitated. "You can, Jan, but Mr. Smith hasn't been feeling that great. He just came home from the hospital and he's got some things in there, some helper things."

I was desperate. "Oh, that's OK. If you don't mind, I don't mind. I'll just ignore them."

Pulling in my tummy and tightening my glutes, I squeezed between the bathroom door and Mr. Smith's walker. It was after I closed the door that I spotted the disabled person's commode perkily perched atop the toilet seat.

Nuts. Do I remove the entire apparatus or simply sit on it? With no time for niceties, I sat down. Hey, good choice. It was comfy and I tucked this information away for *my* future golden years.

While traveling with Dave to our sixth dog, I thought about some of the lavatories of our wealthier clients. I had entered homes where the palatial powder rooms could host a staff meeting for ten. The term "restroom" truly applied to these sanctuaries, and rest I did while sitting and admiring their decor. Fancy soaps, deluxe paper guest towels not found on Sam's Club shelves, gold plated fixtures, pricey wallpaper and delightful aromas were common in these mini-mansions. I mentally tucked away several ideas I could appropriate to spruce up my own restroom.

These were also the homes where I seldom met the owner, but was on a first name basis with the housekeeper.

"Hi, Sarah. It's that time again to groom Samson."

"Mornin', Jan. Mrs. Hess left some notes here about how she wants Samson groomed."

"I'll take a look, but could I possibly use your restroom before I get started?"

"Sure thing, but I haven't cleaned in there yet."

"Oh, I don't care," I said, and I didn't. I was well aware that Sarah cleaned Mrs. Hess' bathroom on a daily basis.

The one drawback to servicing wealthy clients was that they usually didn't tip. I presumed they figured I was just one of their hired help. Then again, their checks didn't bounce, and I always enjoyed the use of their lavatories.

Perhaps Dave wouldn't even notice the grandeur of some bathrooms; I guessed I was more interested from a female viewpoint. However, I did want to pass on advice about our less affluent clients as we headed back to Base.

When it came to bathrooms, the contrast between the rich and the poor was striking. But the less fortunate customers loved their pets just as much as people of means, and sometimes treated their dogs to haircuts before themselves. For these city folks who didn't own cars, a mobile grooming service cost less than hailing a cab, if they could even find one that allowed transporting their pet.

Many customers were employed in service industries. Well acquainted with the importance of tips, they were generous, even with me—the owner. I appreciated their business and tried to give them a price break or offer them "only for today, five dollars off."

I didn't tell my son that in some of those homes, bathroom amenities lost out to more basic requirements. Many toilets didn't feature a seat and failed to flush properly. Earthy aromas replaced the exotic scents of the rich. After spending my day in poorer neighborhoods, I viewed my own home as a glorious palace. The two extremes kept me firmly grounded in my middle class status.

Dave interrupted me, "Isn't it dangerous for us to go into those areas? Why do we still service them, Mom?"

"I actually have two reasons. One is because we've been grooming these dogs for many years, and over time, their neighborhoods have deteriorated. I feel sorry for the older folks who can't just move out. I can't bring myself to leave them in the lurch. The other reason is you'll find those customers are well aware their neighborhood's not the best, and if they see something happening, they'll charge right out of their home to run the questionable character off. I never felt threatened, unless you count a few bottles thrown at the van. And you know what? I just thought of a third reason. I can't imagine anyone in his right mind trying to rob a groomer in a van knowing someone has a dog plus sharp scissors in there!"

"So, Mom, Canine Clippers has never been held up?"

"Nope. Well, actually we were once. The groomer had left her purse on the passenger's seat with the window open. Someone walked by, lifted it and ran. But we weren't even in a questionable neighborhood, so I don't think that counts."

We were almost back to Base and I was reminiscing about one more pit stop story, but being Dave's mom, I was a little embarrassed.

There was the time when my engine quit and the van coasted to a stop. I checked the gas gauge—half full. Was the motor overheating? No. Whatever the problem was, I knew I couldn't fix it and had to call Niel for help.

I was irritated that I hadn't stopped at The Country Deli to use their restroom. I thought it could wait until I reached the next client. Wrong! Today, there would be no next client.

My rescuer wouldn't arrive for half an hour and a certain urgency was developing in my lower regions. Where to find relief? I checked out the suburban homes around my unexpected parking pad. All had never-ending driveways and in my pressing condition, the chances were slim I'd make it to a home, and even if I did, would you welcome a stranger smelling and looking like an escapee from a dog pound?

There was only one solution. Hoping a good Samaritan didn't stop and ask if I needed assistance, I drew the drapes, locked the doors and balanced my buns on the ledge of the bathing tub. "Balanced" was the operative word here, as this was not your typical, firm, round seating. Disaster lurked if I misjudged and slid too far backward or forward. If I guessed correctly and perched just right, I was in business. Even though no one could see me I was uncomfortable and embarrassed. This was not the way my mother raised me! Still, I rationalized, it was an emergency, and if excited dogs could pee in the tub, so could I.

Niel arrived to find me munching an apple, engrossed in my book and seemingly quite happy to abandon the rest of my route that day.

He asked, "Everything OK?"

"Just hunky-dory."

I didn't mention that little episode to Dave. I figured if he encountered a similar situation, he'd find his own pit stop—such as a convenient bush. Come to think of it, he probably wouldn't care as much as I did about those nasty gas station restrooms either.

12

Baubles, Bangles and Beads

In the dog grooming world, baubles, bangles and beads translated into bows, bandanas and cologne. Customer complaints could have been cut in half if we had simply bathed, brushed, dried and made dogs look good without adding the extras. Finishing touches sometimes became more important than the actual grooming. But those extras made all the difference to the client, and had an enormous effect on the size of the tip. They were here to stay.

Take bows. I may have spent twenty extra minutes fine-scissoring the puff on Miss Muffin's topknot while she jerked her head from side to side, but all that effort went down the drain if I forgot to attach perky ribbons. If Sporty wasn't sporting a bandana around his neck, his miffed master was sure to notice. And if I forgot to spritz cologne on him…aaagh! Whatever beauty item I omitted usually meant a trip back to the van for a redo.

One day, Mrs. J. Winston III, known as Cynthia to me, phoned with a special request. "My daughter Penny is getting married next Saturday. I'd like my three little Yorkshire terriers groomed on Friday. Now, it's important they have purple ribbons to match the bridesmaid dresses."

"That shouldn't be a problem," I assured her. "We've several shades of purple available."

The day before the wedding when Rhonda arrived, Mrs. Coleman's ten-year-old daughter was the only family member at home. Rhonda asked her, "What shade of purple would your mother like?" The child had no clue. Rhonda made an executive decision and chose a royal purple. After perfectly grooming the little cuties, she toted the pups back to their home and moved on to her next appointment before returning to Base.

Around five that afternoon I received a frantic call from Cynthia. "Rhonda used the wrong shade of purple. How could she? Tell her to get back here and do it right."

I said, "But Mrs. Coleman, you weren't home to show her the correct shade. You could have left one of the bridesmaid's dresses out so Rhonda could match the color." I concluded in my firm, most businesslike voice, "And besides, Rhonda has left for the day."

Unimpressed by my explanation, Cynthia launched into "in-charge" mother-of-the-bride mode—higher pitch and volume. "I don't care. This is the most important day in my daughter's life and I want those bows changed to the right shade! Send someone else out!"

Since Cynthia was a steady customer and usually not that picky, I figured her panic was due to the momentous occasion. I sighed, acutely aware the "someone else" would be me. When the last van arrived back at Base that afternoon, I checked to make sure it was stocked with every imaginable shade of purple ribbon and hopped in. I was not in a pleasant mood as I traveled to Cynthia's.

Cynthia had alerted me that she would be at the rehearsal dinner, but would leave her door unlocked. This time she remembered to leave a swatch of bridesmaid dress material wrapped around one of the Yorkie's collar. I gently plucked the offending royal purple ribbons from their ears and attached soft lavender ones. I couldn't stop giggling as I pictured the Yorkies, one by one, marching down the church aisle. Or perhaps each bridesmaid would carry one in her arms instead of a bouquet. Either way, the pups' and bridesmaids' shades of purple would be a perfect match. Mission accomplished.

The most astounding request for ribbons occurred on the day I pulled up at a funeral home. I was certain I had the wrong address and was ready to move on when someone knocked on the van window. As I rolled it down, I recognized Frankie, a little white Maltese, being held by the client's daughter.

"Jan, I know this is a bit unusual, but Mom's funeral is this afternoon and I know she would want Frankie looking his best. And Jan," (I know you've guessed what came next) "would you put black bows on his ears?"

Without missing a beat, I asked, "Would you like a black bandana to match?" and the instant the words came out of my mouth, I realized this was not the proper moment to be sarcastic.

She swallowed and said, "Yes, how sweet of you to think of that; Mom would have loved it."

Thank you, Lord. She failed to notice my foot-in-mouth gaffe.

Praying the arriving mourners wouldn't trip over the electric cord I stretched between the van and funeral home, I gave Frankie his best-ever grooming. Fortunately, we stocked a few black accessories for Halloween and New Year's Eve. As I attached the black bows sprinkled with silver glitter onto his ears, and tied a matching bandana around his neck, I wondered what role Frankie played in the funeral. Would he be positioned near the coffin to receive condolences with the other mourners? Was he a pallbearer trotting alongside the casket? When they reached the cemetery, would he get the urge to pee—somewhere?

Oh, it was just too, too bizarre, and although inappropriate, I couldn't stop chuckling. I recovered long enough to thank the daughter for the $100 tip and briefly considered expanding my business into a little known niche specializing in grooming a dog for its owner's funeral. Perhaps I was even ahead of the Hollywood trendsetters, but since that was the sole funeral in which a pet played a significant role in my twenty-one years as a groomer, there couldn't have been much of a market.

However, there were several other unusual cases in which an owner planned to have an elderly pet euthanized and asked me to groom him before the trip to the vet. No way would I be able to groom and blubber at the same time. I expressed my sympathy and declined.

Canine Clippers stocked the vans with seasonal ribbons for all occasions. In spring we attached white ribbons printed with little green shamrocks. Summer called for daisies or pink and lavender flowers; fall brought out gold bows featuring turkeys or brown leaves. Come winter, we supplied ribbons with snowflakes and candy canes.

Groomers were often hard-pressed to figure out which holiday the family celebrated. The safest course was simply to ask, but sometimes the owner wasn't home. In those cases, the groomer picked up hints from last names, decorations, the housekeeper, her own previous knowledge, and when all else failed—just gave it her best shot.

But occasionally a groomer had to guess at the religion of the dog. Yes, you read that right.

One Christmas, after Bonnie attached Santa bows to Mr. Henry's miniature poodle's ears, her customer protested, "My dog is not Christian!" Bonnie must have misread the clue of a house embellished with Christmas decorations. Perhaps it was a mixed marriage in which one spouse didn't celebrate the holiday, while the other festooned their home with red and green decorations. Or perhaps the dog simply was not of the same faith as the owner—hard to tell.

Holidays weren't our only downfall in gracing a dog with the wrong ribbons. I arrived at a home where the clients owned a white standard poodle called Sam. Since Mrs. Van Horn wasn't home, I checked with Maddy, their housekeeper, whether the family wanted a bow on his collar. She supposed they did and I attached a huge bright blue one. As he pranced about the van, he seemed to recognize how stunning he looked. With head held high, he was eager to show off to his family.

While leading Sam from the van, I watched a small boy step off his school bus. He spotted Sam and began running toward him. His eyes opened wide and he abruptly stopped. Dropping his backpack, he burst into tears.

"Sam's a boy dog!" he howled. "He doesn't wear bows!"

"Yes, I know he's a boy dog, but Maddy told me to put a big bow on him." (I had learned, just as baby boys were never dressed in pink, male dogs were never adorned in girlie colored bows.)

It was not a big deal. If bows could be attached, they could be un-attached. Why the fuss?

Nonetheless, he ran into the house screaming, "Mommy, Mommy! Sam has a bow on his collar! The lady turned him into a girl dog!" (Talk about power; I could change a dog's sex! Could this be marketable?)

In the meantime, Mrs. Van Horn had returned home. Upon hearing her son's shouts of dismay, she hurried out to smooth things over.

"I'll just remove Sam's bow," I offered.

"I'm so sorry. I guess you better do that. My son thinks you turned Sam into a girl. He's inconsolable."

Off came the bow. Sam didn't care one way or the other. When I led him into his home, I received a very generous tip for participating in the drama.

Back in the van, I wrote a note on Sam's file in large red letters: "NO BOWS! BIG TIPPER!"

Every groomer has his or her unique method of attaching bows to a dog's ears. Rhonda, our champion bow maker, used her talent to create works of art. She didn't simply fashion beautiful bows out of various shades of colors, she also tucked little flowers or tiny holiday objects in their centers. Rhonda's bows were marvelously upscale, out-of-the-ordinary creations and her pleased customers rewarded her with liberal tips.

Rhonda's greatest achievement, however, was that her bows remained attached. In fact, in one case she had fastened them so well, that when she returned three months later, they were still firmly on Mrs. Simmon's toy poodle's ears—although they bore no resemblance to the original, attractive, plump bows.

Rhonda advised, "You really need to remove these ribbons from Queenie's ears after a few days."

Mrs. Simmons said, "But she looked so cute," and tacked on, "Besides, I was afraid to try to get them out. They seemed to be in there awfully tight."

Rhonda began the tedious job of snipping the ribbons from Queenie's ears to avoid creating a bald spot. On one side, the ear, hair and ribbon had become one huge matted mess. She was appalled when she discovered the rubber band had cut into Queenie's ear, and tourniquet-style, had cut off her circulation. The dog was in danger of losing her ear. Rhonda terminated the grooming and urged, "Mrs. Simmons, you need to take Queenie to a vet immediately to surgically remove the ingrown rubber band."

Mrs. Simmons was having none of it. "This is your fault, Rhonda. You shouldn't have put them in so tight."

Yep, several days later we received an outrageous vet bill. Thereafter, we cautioned owners to remove the ribbons *and* rubber bands within two weeks of their pet's grooming.

One groomer, Frank, had the opposite problem. Even though several of his female co-workers tried to teach him *Bow Making 101,* he never quite developed the knack for creating or attaching them to stay on the dog's ears. He'd barely left a client's home when my phone would ring.

"Sugar's ribbons have fallen out. Send that groomer back!"

When I called Frank, I heard him groan. Both he and I knew that even if he redid the bows, Sugar would shake them loose before the van turned the corner. He became increasingly hopeless about his abysmal bow creations and ever mastering this all-important aspect of the trade.

Befuddled, he commissioned our genius bow maker, Rhonda, to design and show him how to correctly attach bows so they wouldn't slip off. Frank was happy, Rhonda made a few bucks, and from then on, Frank's clients thought he was outstanding.

Then there were bandanas! Ahh, bandanas! Canine Clippers did not usually supply doggie bandanas, but some of the groomers loved to purchase or sew them for their special clients. The lady groomers especially enjoyed giving the pups that extra caring touch. Plus, the pet's owners loved them and were considerably more generous with tips. (Have you noticed how "tips" became the underlying motive for turning out a perfect product *with* the extras?)

The problem arose when a different groomer showed up who didn't stock bandanas. Dave related his experience with a customer who expected one to be hugging his dog's neck.

"Where's his bandana?" Mr. Ernst demanded.

"I don't have any. We guys don't make them. I've got bows. Want one on his collar?"

"What do you mean, you don't make bandanas? He's a male dog—he doesn't get bows. If Max doesn't get a bandana, you should reduce your fee."

"Uh, I can't do that, Mr. Ernst. The charge is the same."

"Well, don't you show up here, again. I want one of the girls. They always put a bandana on Max."

Dave was relieved because the incident was over, but crestfallen because he knew, without peeking, that Mr. Ernst's check wouldn't include a tip.

Most owners expected their pets to smell like Chanel No. 5 when they were returned to them. Generally, shampoo aromas dissipated quickly and experienced groomers spritzed cologne on the dog just before returning it. The vans were stocked with five different selections. Each groomer and client had his or her preference. The dogs hated them all and knew exactly how to rid themselves of these foreign scents.

The scenario usually went like this: Groomer returns Mrs. White's dog, Hank, to its owner. Mrs. White is delighted with Hank's grooming, pays groomer and groomer leaves. Hank has been in the van for over an hour and indicates to Mrs. White he needs to relieve himself. She lets Hank out and he immediately scampers to his favorite backyard peeing place where he rolls around on his back, wriggling back and forth in the urine soaked area until he rids himself of the cologne. Hank now stinks like he thinks a canine should and happily trots back to Mrs. White. She takes one sniff and punches in our phone number.

"Hank smells!" she screams.

I attempt to discover just what "smell" Mrs. White is referring to and ask her, "Could you be more specific?"

"He smells like an outhouse!"

Got it!

I modulate my voice to be calm and soothing and suggest, "The next time Hank is groomed, take him for a walk immediately instead of letting him roam."

However, Hank and I both know he'll find his "special" spot as soon as he's back in his yard. It's our little secret.

Sometimes cologne triggered an allergic reaction in pets or owners and we noted on their records: "Do Not Use Any Scented Products!" But mistakes did happen.

Mrs. Rose, owner of a Scottish terrier named MacDuff, greeted our groomer at the door, "I think MacDuff might be allergic to the cologne you used last time. He scratched and scratched after you left. In fact, I thought maybe he'd picked up a flea from the van." (We tended to dismiss this common complaint—surely not *our* vans.) Mrs. Rose continued, "But I checked him all over and didn't find any. I guess it must be the cologne. Would you note on his file not to use any perfume or cologne?"

Five weeks later Betty again groomed MacDuff. I received a phone call that evening, "I specifically told Betty not to use cologne and now my dog's scratching again. Would you please come out here and bathe him again to get rid of the fragrance? I'm afraid he'll dig himself raw and keep us up all night."

Exhausted from my long day, I nevertheless climbed into the van and drove the half hour to Mrs. Rose's home. Grumbling the entire time and directing evil thoughts Betty's way, I bathed the terrier with odorless shampoo, brushed and dried him again.

I was so peeved with Betty that I was waiting at the door when she strolled in the following morning. "Betty, did you know I had to shampoo MacDuff again last night because you sprayed him with cologne?"

She protested, "But I *didn't* spray him with anything. His notes said not to."

I phoned his owner, "Betty said she didn't use any cologne on MacDuff yesterday."

After a pause, Mrs. Rose said, "You know, he really didn't smell like cologne when Betty brought him in. But he began scratching immediately."

Now we were both confused.

It was Sherlock Holmes time. I asked, "Do you wear perfume?"

"Yes, I do."

"Is it possible that when you cuddled him, his fur picked up your perfume?"

"Maybe."

"Why don't you spray some on yourself right now and see if he has a reaction."

"Okay."

When the conversation deteriorated to one-word terse responses, I knew I had touched a nerve. The next time Betty groomed MacDuff and returned him to his home, Mrs. Rose said, "I never realized my cologne was affecting MacDuff's allergy problem. I've stopped using it. In fact, he doesn't seem to scratch at all anymore."

When Betty told me that, I thought, again, I should be charging detective fees for solving mysteries.

There was one beauty extra that mobile groomers generally didn't add that salons did: nail polish. Could you imagine the problems with incorrect shades, the extra thirty minutes required for drying, and tiny dog hairs glued to wet nails? No, thank you, unless, of course, we clocked extra time and charged thirty dollars more. Drat! Wish I'd thought of that earlier.

13

Employee of the Month

Canine Clippers had been running fairly smoothly for some time. Oh, sure, employees came and went, and the vans continued to be an ongoing pain, but generally I enjoyed the day-to-day managing. There was one chore that I begrudgingly had continued to do myself, however, and that was the weekly van cleaning. For some insane reason, I thought the groomers would tidy up and clean their own vans. Not, so.

Evenings, when they pulled in and charged out of them, half the floating dog hair followed—but not all. Sunday afternoons found Niel and me cleaning vans. By the time five vans were going out six days a week, I realized the job of keeping them hair-free and somewhat sanitary was too much for us, and so I hired a weekend van cleaner. Since free labor (our children) had flown the coop, I turned to the neighborhood kids.

"James," I said, "we need someone to clean the vans on Sundays and we'll pay twenty dollars per van. Would you be interested in the job?"

"Mrs. Nieman, would I ever! Don't ask anyone else. I'm your man."

"My man" lasted about four weeks before he discovered it took five hours to do a decent job instead of the two he had counted on. I personally thought that one hundred bucks was a generous wage for sixteen-year-olds, but it became obvious they valued their weekends off as much as I did. I probably went through most of the neighborhood teens before Lindsay came along.

Lindsay had been one of our groomers, but never picked up enough speed to groom six dogs a day. He went on to a job as a medical equipment driver. However, he wanted to earn a little extra cash to go back to college. We'd leave for church on Sunday mornings, and when we arrived back home, Lindsay was halfway through the task. What a thrill to regain our Sundays, and Lindsay enjoyed working at his leisure. Plus, the groomers appreciated finding a clean van waiting for them on Mondays. Good vibes for everyone.

Those vans went through hell. Groomers were hard on them. Sides were scraped and roof vents sliced off by low-hanging tree branches. Sometimes drivers backed into anything or anyone foolish enough to park behind them—including garage doors and trees.

Our vans originally had a spare tire mounted on the rear just in case a groomer had a flat. After the fifth time a groomer backed into some immovable object and we had a body shop repair the dented door, we removed the tire. The odds were they would back into something else before they had a flat. And we were right. In twenty-one years we never had a flat tire on the road.

Garage gutters were a different story. Our van's raised roof frequently caught on the gutter's edge and ripped it off. Niel became as adept in finding the cheapest place in town for gutter replacements as he was for van parts.

Many groomers were great with dogs, but had questionable driving skills. Patty, a fairly new groomer with Canine Clippers, was a bit apprehensive about driving a van.

"Miz Nieman," she volunteered, "I haven't been driving real long and my car's a little thing."

I was one groomer short and tended to overlook minor red flags. I figured she'd learn. How bad could she be?

"Patty," I assured her, "it's just like driving a slightly larger car. It won't be long before you'll get real comfortable in it."

One month later and long after I presumed she had adjusted, she lost control of the van on the Baltimore Beltway, did a complete U-turn and headed back into oncoming traffic. The first I knew about the incident was when one of her fellow travelers pulled over to the shoulder and phoned. "Your idiot driver is going the wrong way on the beltway!"

The angel sitting on Patty's shoulder sprang into action. The van dodged the oncoming cars and came to a 180-degree stop, facing oncoming traffic, snug against the concrete divider. Frightened by that episode, she resigned, but years later reapplied for a job. When I asked to see her driver's license, she couldn't produce one and admitted it had been revoked. She wasn't rehired. I didn't make that same mistake twice.

Robert, a self-assured groomer but too aggressive a driver, tried to park his van in an underground garage. When the vehicle smashed into the garage's low-hanging supports, he revved it up trying to force it in. Yep, in it went, but only part of the way. After the hysterical tow truck driver collected himself, he let some air out of all four tires and deposited it in Mike's parking lot. Crestfallen, Robert rode back with the tow truck and quit. And yes, we had to replace the entire roof of the van, including the air conditioner sitting on its top. But what bummed me out even more was the $1,500 bill for repairing the garage's concrete struts.

I never dreamed that one of my side duties as an employer was to be a matchmaker. After all, my employees worked alone and often went days without bumping into a co-worker.

Joey, a young, handsome applicant was proud that he hailed from Brooklyn. He was quick to let me know Baltimore didn't measure up to his hometown. He bragged, "Dog groomers here don't make the money they do in Brooklyn."

Shooting back my two cents worth, I said, "Well, Joey, maybe they don't, but you can actually live in Baltimore on what you earn."

On the day that Joey accompanied me to demonstrate his grooming skills, the schedule didn't include a wide selection of breeds. Although I couldn't properly evaluate his abilities, he did show himself to be a people person as he chatted away with owners. But I was uncomfortable hiring him based on a small sampling of dogs. The following day I sent him out with Sheila, one of our younger groomers, and asked her to give me feedback on his expertise.

When they returned, the two were in high spirits—giggling and flirting.

"Well, how'd it go, Sheila?" I asked after Joey left.

"Oh, Jan, he's really good. I think you should hire him. He sure knows how to charm the customers."

It was apparent that Sheila was equally charmed by Joey. They began dating.

Unfortunately, while spending a marvelous day bonding, Sheila hadn't been too critical in observing Joey's clipping and scissoring, because numerous complaints about "how my dog looks," began to filter in. I followed up with a few quality control phone calls, and to my dismay, I found we had lost all of the clients whose dogs Joey had groomed. I subsequently discovered he had fibbed about his previous experience and was definitely not "Employee of the Month" material.

I never discovered whether my besotted groomer found out if Joey lacked other skills. When I fired him after three weeks, she also resigned, and there went another groomer—or in effect, two.

After hiring many inept groomers, I was ecstatic when I found one who not only loved working with animals, but could keep a van on the road without incident. If an applicant's grooming aptitude matched his or her driving skills, I was quick to overlook personal idiosyncrasies.

When Karen arrived for her interview, I was taken aback by her shaved head, eyebrow rings and a dozen earring studs. She later confided she had nipple jewelry as well, which no one had a chance to confirm or admire. The other groomers and I speculated her missing hair was due to cancer treatments. After several months, during which it never grew longer than half an inch, I finally worked up enough nerve to ask.

She said, "It's too much bother to keep up with haircuts. I just have my boyfriend run a #7 blade over it every few weeks."

To each her own! If nothing else, it cut down on long discussions when a customer couldn't recall her name. They'd say, "I want that groomer with the bald head."

Karen became a proficient, dependable and compassionate groomer. The only complaint we received was that she went overboard lecturing customers when their dogs were in poor shape. She wasn't trying to be mean. She simply wouldn't overlook even minor pet neglect and sometimes threatened owners with SPCA action. The phrase "the customer is always right" didn't hold any weight with Karen.

In time I discovered her unique lifestyle. She owned an old farmhouse back in the woods, complete with an army of feral cats. Karen, friend to all animals, housed a snake in her walls. It didn't bother her as long as it left the cat militia alone. When sportsmen requested permission to hunt on her property, they were promptly booted off. No animal died on her watch. Needless to say, she was a vegetarian.

A creek ran through her property, and when it flooded, she was stranded due to the lack of a bridge. One morning after an all-night downpour, my phone rang at 6:00 a.m. "Jan, this is Karen. The creek came up last night and I can't get over. Call my customers and I'll get in as soon as it recedes."

If she was already at work when the flood came, she played musical beds with friends who took her in for the night until the water went down.

In mid-December, she frowned when I gave her the next week's schedule. Pouting, she said, "I never get off on *my* holiday."

I drew a blank. "What is your holiday, Karen?" I was aware that Hanukkah, Christmas and Kwanzaa fell close to one another. Was there one I was overlooking?

She said, "My religion celebrates the winter solstice. Just once in a while I'd like to have off on *my* holiday."

Sometimes we could accommodate her, other times, not. Eventually grooming became too strenuous for her and she was forced to resign. But you know what? In a snip of a hair, I'd hire Karen again.

In truth, we didn't bestow an award for "Employee of the Month." But if we did, that person would have outstanding groomer skills, a talent for excellent public relations and be a decent driver. Add to that a pleasant personality, initiative and trustworthiness—someone who wouldn't take advantage of sick or annual leave.

Enter Rodney.

Rodney arrived promptly for his interview. Already, I was impressed. As soon as he stepped into the office, I recognized him. It would have been hard to forget him—a six-foot-tall, muscular, good-looking African American with a nice smile and natural charm. He had previously applied for a grooming position, and at his initial interview accompanied me for a day to demonstrate his grooming skills. They had been exceptional. However, his hours of availability and our hours of operation conflicted because he drove his eight-year-old daughter to school.

Here he was, applying again.

So," I asked, "has the situation with your daughter changed? Are you more flexible?"

"Yes, I am. Tanesha's old enough to walk with her friends now."

"Well, Rodney, you already showed me you're an above average groomer, but there's one thing holding me back from hiring you."

Surprised, he asked, "What's that?"

"When you applied before, I checked your references with your former employers. They all said you were a great groomer, but you were habitually tardy, and on some days you didn't show up at all. One told me that after one of your absences, you arrived the next day wearing a brand-new, neatly creased 'Atlantic City' T-shirt."

Rodney leaned back on his chair's two rear legs, folded his hands over his chest and mulled this over. "That's not exactly right. I needed to take my daughter to school, so I had an arrangement with the salon owner to come in later than the other groomers."

He took a moment to think about what he'd said, and clarified, "I did leave when I was done with my dogs, which was usually before the other groomers finished. I always got my work done, and I know my clients were satisfied with the way I groomed their dogs. Now that I think about it, when you made that call, I doubt you spoke to the owner, but to someone who didn't know about the arrangement."

Still skeptical, I asked, "What about the absences, Rodney?"

"Sometimes I took time off when I was getting burned out, but I always phoned in. I don't know about the 'Atlantic City' shirt. I don't remember that."

Some of the bad vibes I had experienced with Eddie came back. I was apprehensive, but I took a chance on Rodney.

During his first month, I checked his work through quality controls, asking his clients the usual questions, "Was your groomer on time? Was he polite? Were you satisfied with the quality of his work?" The responses were unanimous. "Oh, yes. He was not only on time, he called to warn me he was running early. My dog loved him and has never looked better. In fact, I want only Rodney. Please make a note on Buffy's record." Noted!

We had customers who, when I groomed their dog, would make remarks about not sending a male groomer, or a black groomer, or if they were black, to not send a white groomer. I pretty much ignored these comments and scheduled whoever was in their area on the day they wanted. I wasn't about to play that game. If they didn't like it, they could take their business elsewhere.

Mrs. Peyton, an older client who owned an apricot-colored miniature poodle, Sunshine, lived in a well-preserved Victorian home. The area suggested "old" money and at one time was the crème de la crème for Baltimore society. Mrs. Peyton was picky about Sunshine's grooming, but always waited until the last minute to schedule an appointment.

Rodney had the first opening, and I sent him.

Later that day Mrs. Peyton phoned. "Jan, don't you warn people when you send them a black groomer?"

"Ah, no. Why would I do that?"

"Well, I sure was surprised when this big, black guy showed up," she said. I waited for the other shoe to drop, when she continued, "but he is the best groomer I've ever had. You can send him anytime!"

The compliments were so over the top, I suspected Rodney bribed his clients to phone in rave reviews (although I couldn't figure out what the incentive would be).

After three months, Rodney had more requests for his services than the other four groomers combined. They were just as talented and good with customers, but Rodney had an infectious smile and seldom lost his temper. He disarmed unhappy customers by redoing a dog that another groomer had incorrectly groomed, and he didn't charge them or us for his extra effort.

Canine Clippers had one client, Mrs. Ackerman, who was picky to the nth degree. Several groomers refused to return because they spent way too much time traipsing back and forth to the van with Pepsi, her miniature poodle, to trim a little more here, a little more there.

The next time Mrs. Ackerman scheduled an appointment for Pepsi, I placed him on Rodney's route. When he arrived, he was met on the doorstep by Mr. Ackerman.

He said, "Before you groom Pepsi, I want to tell you something about my wife. She's a little difficult to get along with, but she's the love of my life. Just do anything she wants, and I guarantee you'll be very happy with your tip."

After Rodney brought her dog back, Mrs. Ackerman looked Pepsi over with a fine-tooth comb (literally), but unable to find any fault, she paid him. True to his word, Mr. Ackerman came around from the side of the house and slipped Rodney ten bucks.

Rodney didn't mind one bit dealing with the missus, especially when he was so handsomely rewarded. Mrs. Ackerman always asked for him, and after each grooming, her husband snuck over with Rodney's bonus.

One day Mrs. Ackerman phoned for an appointment and I could tell she was distraught. Her husband had passed away. After I expressed my condolences, she scheduled an appointment with Rodney. He did his usual great job, but this time Mrs. Ackerman found all sorts of things wrong. She also asked Rodney to plug his electrical cord in at the neighbor's condo as she didn't want to leave her door partially open.

The neighbors were a bit put out because now *their* door was open a crack. But since Mrs. Ackerman had just lost her husband, they made allowances. She became ever more demanding and never tipped for the extra time Rodney spent there trying to please her.

One day I asked him, "How come you continue to groom Mrs. Ackerman's dog?"

He said, "Because that could be my mother some day and I'd want people to treat her with respect. Besides, she doesn't have Mr. Ackerman there anymore to protect her, she's lonely, and I figure this is the least I can do." That was Rodney.

Most groomers arrived around 7:30 to begin their day. Rodney popped in at 7:00. We'd chat, sip coffee, and he'd help start the five vans. If a water line was frozen, he held the hair dryer while I fumbled around in the dark to locate the offending piece of ice. When he saw me struggling with a problem, he never failed to ask, "How can I help?"

Contrary to his previous employer's warning, Rodney proved to be dependable and never absent unless he was ill—a rare occurrence. He scheduled his vacations months ahead of time, eliminating inconveniencing both his clients and me.

One morning when we were chatting, he mentioned that he was concerned about his two stepsons' education after high school. It was then I discovered he hadn't finished high school himself. School had been difficult and he drifted, as many Baltimore kids did.

"Jan," he said, "do you know how I got to be a dog groomer?"

"I haven't a clue. How?"

"I snagged a job washing dogs when I was fourteen, and I watched everything the groomer did. Pretty soon I was clipping nails and cleaning out ears. One day the groomer didn't show up. We had a whole bunch of dogs sitting in cages, and I just started in on them. The owner thought I did a pretty decent job, and after that I got to be a groomer."

We developed a relationship that was more mother/son than employer/employee. I was curious as to why a man with his talent didn't have his own grooming shop. Months after we became comfortable speaking about most any topic, I asked him, "Rodney, did you ever consider starting your own business?"

"Sure." He set down his coffee cup and looked out the window. I could tell he was debating whether to continue.

His voice was softer when he said, "Most people don't know this, but until three years ago, I had a heavy drug problem. Any extra money went for drugs."

"So," venturing further, "how did you get off drugs?"

"I just did. I prayed the Lord would help me and He did and I haven't done drugs since." He swiveled his chair to face me and added, "This is the best job I've ever had. I'm making more money now than I ever did in a grooming shop. It's steady and I don't get laid off."

I had my answer.

Since he had considerably more grooming experience than I did, I assigned new applicants to him for evaluation and trusted his judgment completely. If he cautioned me not to hire someone, I didn't. If he approved them, that person became part of Canine Clipper's family. I often wished I would have hired his clone twenty-one years earlier.

At least I was fortunate to have employed this ex-addict for my last four years, and he remained a friend. Unlike Willie and Eddie, who also were outstanding groomers, Rodney conquered his addiction and not only survived, but excelled.

He definitely would have been named Canine Clippers' Employee of the Month!

14

Horror "Tails"

Misunderstandings about beauty extras were a minor dilemma compared to injuries that could happen during a grooming. Sometimes a cat or dog harmed a groomer; other times it was the reverse. Wounds inflicted on a groomer usually healed fast and didn't involve a dash to the emergency room. I wish I could say the same for pets, but we received our share of vet bills for injuries we caused on the job. I'm reluctant to "fess up" to some of those, but since I did promise to tell all—here goes.

Groomers didn't intentionally hurt pets. Most loved animals, or they wouldn't have chosen a profession that came with the occasional nip and nick. I'll admit that there were those times when my first reaction to a dog biting or scratching me was to retaliate in kind. Of course, I never did, and neither did the groomers I hired. But the longer they were on the job, the greater were the odds that they would accidentally hurt a pet.

With new groomers, I made a point of telling them to always advise owners if they injured their animals. I also told them, if it did happen, to let me know immediately. Some did, some didn't.

"Amy," I said after an unpleasant phone conversation with a client, "...anything you want to mention about what happened at the Johnsons'?"

"Oh, I forgot to tell you about that. Mr. Johnson didn't let me know that Bubbles had a large growth behind his ear. The clipper took it right off."

Amy looked suitably contrite and I told her again, "Never try to cover up an accident. We all have them, but I need to know immediately, and not hear about it from an outraged client first."

One time I received an unusually large bill from a vet for a dog Ursula had groomed several weeks earlier. Waving it in front her, I asked, "What's this all about?"

"Oh my," she said after scanning it, "I guess Mrs. Barnsworth took Inky to the vet after all. I wasn't going to mention it, because it didn't seem like a big deal at the time."

"Oh, really?"

"I snipped the tip of his penis, but he didn't whine or do anything, and there wasn't much blood either."

It took a lot for me to lose my temper, but that did it. I fired Ursula. I also deducted half of the vet bill from her final paycheck. And predictably, Mrs. Barnsworth did not remain a Canine Clippers client.

I'll admit I had my own share of pet accidents. Take nail clipping. I cringed when I reached that part of the grooming. Even after years of experience, it was always a guessing game of "how much nail can I trim back before I hit a vein?"

My experience with Hans, a miniature schnauzer, was unforgettable (have you noticed schnauzers were my Achilles' heel?). Mr. Hill, Hans' owner, lived in a new development of beautiful condos with underground parking. These were fine homes with exquisite furniture and carpeting. Mr. Hill's unit was halfway down a long walk, so I used all two hundred feet of electrical extension cords to reach his power outlet.

He handed his dog to me and I marched Hans to the van. He was fairly cooperative for most of his grooming until I reached for a paw. He growled. Being a typical terrier with nail sensitivity, Hans was telling me, "Don't you even think about touching my nails."

Securing a muzzle around his jaws, I used every grooming know-how trick to get the job done. I tucked his head and neck under my armpit facing away from me, and mustering all my strength to keep him there, trimmed all sixteen nails in record time. I gently placed grumpy Hans on the floor, swept up his grey clippings and cleaned the grooming area.

With a lead around Hans' neck and ready to take this handsome dog back to his owner, I noticed red spots on the floor.

I was pretty certain I hadn't nicked Hans. Therefore, I reasoned, the blood had to be oozing from one of his hard-fought-over nails. Ugh! Neither of us was thrilled when I lifted him back to the grooming table. To my dismay, *four* nails were bleeding—one on each paw.

Hans and I had already fought Round One over his nails. I picked up a paw and Hans growled again. On went the muzzle. I applied a product created to stop the bleeding and waited for it to live up to its reputation. I waited, applied, waited, applied, and waited some more. Twenty minutes passed before I was satisfied it had done its magic. Not willing to chance another outbreak when a nail touched concrete, I carried Mr. Grumpy back down that long sidewalk to his home.

Mr. Hill waited at his open door, arms folded across his chest, apparently annoyed that Hans' grooming had taken so long. He grudgingly acknowledged, "Well, he looks terrific."

"Thank you," I said, and not mentioning the battle over nails, fibbed, "he's a good dog."

While I gingerly lowered Hans to the entryway, Mr. Hill wrote out a check. Released, and clearly on cloud nine now that he was back in his home, Hans joyfully bounded into the living room. His owner and I beamed at one another. Wasn't he a good-looking pup? Wasn't he just the best?

At that moment Mr. Hill spotted drops of red on his light grey carpeting, "What's that?"

I followed his pointing finger, and in spite of all my precautions, Hans' nails had broken open again.

Mr. Hill hurried to snatch up his bleeding pup. Game for a chase, Hans raced into the dining room, ran under the table, shot out the other side, jumped to the couch, leaped to a chair and bounced back to the carpet, leaving a trail of blood everywhere. I watched in awe as the two of them raced through the house.

Mr. Hill yelled, "My furniture, my carpeting, my dog!" (Notice the priorities?)

I screamed along, "Get him! Get him!"

In no time, the grey carpeting and beautiful, stylish white furniture became streaked with blood—a murder scene right out of "CSI."

Mr. Hill finally cornered Hans and grabbed him. His previously immaculate white shirt looked as though a pint of red paint had been tipped down its front. He handed Hans to me, and after placing a lead around his neck, I hustled him back to the van. We hung out for another miserable thirty minutes until I was positive his nails wouldn't bleed again. I was now more than an hour late for my next appointment and phoned the client to cancel. This was going to be a costly affair.

When I returned with his dog, Mr. Hill narrowed his eyes and frowned. His mouth was puckered as though he had just bitten into a sour pickle. I apologized, did not charge for the grooming, and asked him to obtain an estimate for furniture and carpet cleaning. Several days later the bill arrived. Those damages, plus the loss of income from his and the cancelled appointment, totaled over seven hundred dollars.

Mr. Hill never used our services again. I wouldn't have either.

Every groomer encountered dogs so severely matted it was difficult to determine where the skin ended and the hair began. These pets did not remain unscathed when you employed an Edward Scissorhands approach. Better to oh-so-carefully edge that clipper and scissors through the hair. This was not the time for speed.

Customers assured us that they brushed their dogs daily, but neglected to mention it was done with a soft tool that skimmed over the top coat, leaving a huge matted, solid mass beneath. In those cases it took an experienced, careful groomer to clip the hair off without nicking the animal.

Mrs. Lambert, owner of Mickey and Minnie, two little Lhasa apsos, warned me they were severely matted. When I checked them out, I agreed and advised her that my only option was to shave them. I had her sign a form absolving our company of any injury resulting from grooming due to her pets' terrible condition.

As I placed the dogs in the van, she backed her car down the driveway. Rolling down the window, she waved and shouted, "I have to run to the store. I'll be back."

Lhasas have long tails that spiral over their backs. I clipped, bathed and saved Minnie's tail hair by initially cutting through the mats and painstakingly brushing out the fur until it was totally mat-free. I dried this effervescent little girl and placed her on the floor to dance around while I worked on Mickey.

His tail was in much worse condition. As I worked the scissors through his mats, I spotted blood on his fur. He hadn't reacted to a cut. Was the blood mine? Was it his? As I examined both of us, I was horrified to see I had inadvertently sliced into his tightly coiled tail. Horrors!

The slash was deep. I was in a panic. Mrs. Lambert hadn't yet returned, and this injured dog required a veterinarian—fast. I set him on the van floor with Minnie, disconnected my electrical cord, and raced to a local vet as though I was on Mr. Toad's Wild Ride at Disney

World. Carnage ruled inside the van as Mickey's wagging tail spewed blood all over Minnie, the interior and me as well.

When we arrived at the animal hospital, the vet took charge of Mickey and assured me the cut was minor. What did he know? My van looked like a slaughterhouse. He was going to keep him overnight and he would be happy to bill me. For sure!

But how was Mrs. Lambert going to react when I returned with only one dog, and that one blood-covered? I lucked out—she wasn't home yet. After re-bathing and drying Minnie, I wiped her companion's blood off the floor, the seats, the ceiling and me. I could only imagine what would go through Niel's mind when he laundered this batch of towels.

Her owner pulled into the driveway the second I finished attaching gorgeous pink bows in Minnie's remaining ear hair. I spritzed her with cologne and no one would have suspected she had looked like a butcher shop escapee a few minutes earlier.

Mrs. Lambert peeked into the van and asked, "Where's Mickey?"

"Well, actually, Mickey had a little accident. I had to take him to the vet to get a few stitches in his tail."

"Oh?"

Words tumbled out of my mouth, attempting to minimize the incident. "He was so severely matted it was impossible to tell where his hair was attached to his skin. The scissors nicked him." (Not me, you understand, but the scissors.) "I took him to Dr. Chan and he said he could be picked up tomorrow."

Remarkably, Mrs. Lambert wasn't perturbed. I added that I'd be responsible for the vet bill and there would be no charge for this grooming, even though she had signed a release. I'm sure she wouldn't have taken this episode so lightly if she had returned earlier. The bloodbath in my truck could have inspired a Jackson Pollock painting.

I expected she would never use our services again, but I was surprised when she scheduled another appointment. I rewarded her loyalty with one of our "Five Dollars Off" coupons. It was the least I could do.

Betty, one of our most caring, loving groomers, shed tears when she told me what happened to Harvey, an elderly toy poodle.

Sister Anne, a nun and principal of a Catholic elementary school, said Harvey had a throat condition and the vet had warned her that restraints should not be placed around his neck. Betty had groomed Harvey for years and was familiar with his condition. As he aged, he became difficult to control on the grooming table. She solved the dilemma by keeping one hand on him at all times and grooming with the other. He may not have turned out as neat as she would have liked, but it was one of those "best-you-can-do" jobs.

That day, while Betty was grooming Harvey, he stumbled about with abnormally spastic movements. Finished with the tricky process, she turned to the ribbon spool to unfurl enough length for two bows. As she did, she relaxed her grip on Harvey. He tottered to the edge of the grooming table, and before Betty could catch him, tumbled to the floor.

Horrified, she picked him up from the floor and rushed him back to Sister Anne, blurting out, "I looked away for just an instant, and Harvey stepped off the grooming table. I don't know how badly he's hurt, but I think we should take him to the vet."

While Betty drove, Sister Anne cradled Harvey. When they arrived at the vet's, Harvey was unconscious. The vet carried him into the examining room while an apprehensive Sister Anne and Betty waited and consoled each other. An hour later the vet returned to the waiting room with the prognosis.

"I'm going to keep him overnight. I can't tell if he's suffered a concussion, and I'd like to take some X-rays."

Betty was extremely distraught and unable to finish her route. I, too, was upset, not only for Harvey, Sister Anne, and Betty, but also about the momentous vet bill sure to come, possibly followed by a lawsuit.

I called the vet the following day to check on Harvey's condition. The news was not good.

"He hasn't really come around. His neck seems to have been re-injured," he scolded.

Harvey spent a week at the vet's. Each day I called for an update, phoned Sister Anne and kept Betty informed about his condition. We were all worried.

Sister Anne asked, "How could Betty let him fall off the table like that?"

I comforted her, but wishing to defend my employee, added, "Sister Anne, Betty never would deliberately allow Harvey to fall. She's upset over this, too."

Harvey had been at the vet's for two weeks when Sister Anne phoned. Expecting the worst, I inhaled, closed my eyes and asked, "How is Harvey doing?"

Imagine my relief when I heard the joy in her voice. "You'll never believe this. It's a miracle! I'm picking up Harvey today. He's going to be OK!"

Sister Anne blessed us with forgiveness and Canine Clippers was "blessed" with a $1,565 vet bill. We paid it without complaint. Did Betty ever groom Harvey again? No. From then on he was groomed at the vet's where more than one pair of hands was available to hang onto him.

As I said before, grooming a cat was a two-person job (at the best of times) and frequently that meant calling on the client for help. We did so reluctantly. An owner in the van slowed a groomer down and became more of a liability than an asset ("Aren't you hurting Honey when you do that?"). But after a number of disastrous attempts to groom cats without their assistance, we formulated a "cat policy" that requested—no, actually demanded—that the cat's owner be available to lend a hand if it appeared events were skittering out of control.

In once instance, Dave initially tried to groom a feline customer alone, but when Jasmine the cat hissed and clawed him, he realized it wasn't going to work. He asked the owner, Mrs. Chandler, to step into the van and help. Just as he began, Mrs. Chandler's five-year-old grandchild pounded on the door, yelling, "Grandma, come out and play with me."

Both Mrs. Chandler and Dave grabbed the startled Jasmine as she attempted to leap from the table. Despite her grandmother's orders to stop banging on the van door, the child persisted.

Mrs. Chandler apologized as she stepped out of the van. "I'm afraid I won't be able to help you."

Dave turned to Jasmine, not sure what his next step should be. At this point he'd had limited experience with cats, but was willing to give it a try. Jasmine was having none of it. She backed into a corner and hissed. Dave knew he had a wildcat on his hands and placed a noose around her neck to prevent her from jumping off the table. Huge mistake! (I think you can see where this is headed.) Jasmine fought. She twisted. She lunged upward, but Dave doggedly hung on.

He later told me, "She seemed to eventually cooperate, and I thought I had worn down her resistance."

He finished the grooming, but when he picked her up to return her to Mrs. Chandler, she was limp. Her head drooped at an odd angle— not a good sign.

Dave worriedly placed her in Mrs. Chandler's arms. When she stroked Jasmine and the cat didn't respond, Mrs. Chandler's eyes narrowed. "What's the matter with her?"

"I don't really know. She suddenly just gave up fighting."

Dave and Mrs. Chandler were both in a panic as they rushed Jasmine to the vet. While they waited, Mrs. Chandler's silence and hostility were palpable. An hour later, the vet gravely reported, "It appears Jasmine has reinjured her larynx. Her windpipe also has been damaged." He glared at Dave. "What went on here?"

Mrs. Chandler hadn't mentioned Jasmine's earlier neck injury, and during her struggle, the cat had nearly strangled herself. Mrs. Chandler hinted she might contact her attorney, but when we reminded her of her responsibility to stay in the van, she backed down.

But I felt horrible and responsible. Because I had given up on cats, I hadn't fed Dave much information on how to groom them and neglected mentioning to never put a noose around their necks.

A second miracle: Jasmine survived, although she lived out the rest of her days with a brace around her neck. For months we worried about repercussions. I paid the $1,200 veterinarian bill, didn't charge Dave for his half and decided we couldn't afford cats. Jasmine would be the last feline we ever groomed.

Sometimes a groomer became a pet's savior. Ethel, a regular client, was a nervous, tall, thin elderly lady who subsisted on a meager income and Meals on Wheels. Her Chihuahua, Cindy, didn't really need our services, and when Ethel phoned to schedule an appointment, I'd try to talk her out of it.

"Cindy just needs to be brushed every now and then. You could save the expense if you did it yourself."

Ethel was adamant. "But she smells and her skin don't look good. She needs a bath real bad."

So we continued to groom Cindy, but her regular groomer, Rhonda, was concerned with the pup's funky skin. When returning Cindy to the apartment one day, she noticed a strong bleach odor and asked Ethel, "I've noticed that Cindy's skin is peeling. Are you using bleach on your wood floors?"

Ethel said, "Yes, I need to keep everything super clean for Cindy."

Rhonda said, "Oh, Ethel. Cindy's tummy is so close to the floor that I think the bleach is scraping her skin off."

But Ethel wasn't convinced. "No, no. The bleach isn't doing it. She's got a skin condition and the vet told me to keep things clean."

Rhonda asked to see Cindy's medicine, hoping she would discover the vet's name and phone number. We called the vet with our findings. Appalled he said, "My God!" and assured us he would call Ethel to convince her not to clean the floors with bleach anymore.

Several months later, Rhonda was pleased to see Cindy's skin back to normal and the apartment devoid of a bleach odor. Mystery solved, Chihuahua rescued.

There was another situation in which I attempted to convince an owner she was harming her dog with love. Mrs. Fishbein and her mother lived together. They owned and adored their two Chihuahuas, Elmer and Fudd. But after several months of grooming them, I couldn't help but notice that they were gaining a lot of weight around their middles.

I tried to be gentle and tactful as I told Mrs. Fishbein, "I think you might be overfeeding Elmer and Fudd. They're much heavier than they should be."

She didn't disagree. "Oh, I know. It's Mom who's doing it. She sneaks snacks to them all day long and I can't catch her."

I discarded diplomacy and got straight to the point. "Well, these are little fellows and you're shortening their lives with too much food. Please tell your mom she isn't doing them any favors."

Mrs. Fishbein backed up and looked away. I knew I had been harsh but hoped she'd heed my advice and cut down on the extras. But the little guys' bodies continued to grow until they looked like four sticks with a sausage perched on top.

One day, after they were groomed, Mrs. Fishbein told me both dogs were going to undergo knee surgery and have pins inserted so they could walk and hold their weight.

I pleaded with her, "You know, if you fed them less, this wouldn't be happening."

She avoided eye contact and handed me the check.

Mrs. Fishbein's mother and her Chihuahua, Fudd, both died within a few months of each other. I hoped that with her mother gone, Mrs. Fishbein wouldn't overfeed Elmer with doggie goodies and give him a better chance at life. It was not to be. He continued to expand and also died. Although I was sorry to hear Elmer had passed away, I was relieved not to witness the results of Mrs. Fishbein's behavior. But within a week, she purchased another Chihuahua pup and made an appointment to have her groomed.

She and I oohed and aahed over the new arrival, Lolita, and I once again warned her about following a proper diet. The next time I arrived, Lolita was already plumping out around her middle. I looked at this tiny, defenseless pet and feeling anger well up inside me, foresaw her entire future, or lack thereof.

When Mrs. Fishbein phoned for another appointment, I told her, "I'd love to groom Lolita, but not under the circumstances. Unless you promise to take better care of her and keep her weight down, I can't watch your defenseless dog being destroyed."

Mrs. Fishbein hung up and I was in a quandary over what to do about the situation. In Ethel's case we had recourse to contact her vet, and he helped convince her to keep her dog healthy. But was overfeeding really neglect? Surely it was animal abuse. It was a grey area and I just couldn't bring myself to call Mrs. Fishbein's vet, whoever he was. In the end I did nothing. In retrospect, perhaps I should have reported her for animal cruelty and saved Lolita; it's one of the incidents that continues to haunt me.

Most owners loved and treated their pets just fine. If I found they were unintentionally doing something harmful, they generally took my advice and stopped that action (or in the case of not brushing, started the activity). The most frequent cases of "neglect" involved not exercising pets often enough or overfeeding them. Every so often I came across a pet that needed a major teeth cleaning. In those instances I referred the customer to a vet who administered anesthesia and worked with the proper tools.

It wouldn't surprise me if, after reading this chapter about horror "tails," you might consider grooming your little sweetie or your big guy yourself. If this is the point where you decide to purchase scissors, brush and clipper—think again. I don't recommend it. Having seen the results of owners attempting the job on their own, all I can say is, they weren't pretty! Also remember, there's a considerable learning curve. I made more than my fair share of mistakes in my early grooming years, and you, too, with your limited experience, are likely to inflict injuries on your baby. So don't turn your back on professional groomers too quickly. They might be your best bet in taking care of your beloved pet!

15

One Wolf Too Many

· ·

When I started my business, I intended to groom dogs and maybe cats, but not birds, hamsters or rabbits—and definitely not wolves! As uninformed as I was about the various dog breeds when entering this venture, I had no inkling that a mixed breed of wolf and dog even existed. If I had known, I would have thought a veterinarian would be the professional "go to" person for cleaning up a wild animal like that. The possibility that person would be me never even entered my mind.

Along with discovering that wolf-dogs were an accepted pet, I learned that generally men bred them, but when it came to cleaning them, it was a groomer who was called in. Those were the occasions on which I asked myself, "Why, oh why, did I choose this profession?"

In my early years of owning Canine Clippers, when I received a request to groom a wolf mix, I refused. Uh-uh, not me! My training hadn't covered that subject, and it didn't take much of a pet-issued-threat for me to reach my low terror threshold. I wasn't about to take on a wolf, but...

"Jan, I just purchased a cute little mixed breed," Mr. Marshall innocently stated.

"How nice. What sort of mix is she?" I asked.

"She's part husky and part wolf. She really doesn't need much grooming other than a good brushing out and a bath. She's such a placid dog." As a clincher he added, "Canine Clippers does such an amazing job on Brownie, we really want you to groom Kayla, too."

It was, once again, one of those moments when flattery won out over common sense. I scheduled the appointment but—having the advantage of being Canine Clippers' owner—I gave the dog to my groomer Sandy.

One of Kayla's eyes was brown and the other blue. Sandy became unnerved when Kayla continued to maintain eye contact. It was common for dogs to show dominance that way, but when they were in the groomer's territory (in our case, the van), they usually looked away. Kayla didn't. Although she did not become aggressive during her grooming, she spooked Sandy enough that she refused to groom her again.

The next time Mr. Marshall scheduled an appointment for both Kayla and Brownie, I added them to my own route. The fact that Mr. Marshall was a liberal tipper had nothing to do with it—right.

Huskies are members of the working group (think sled dogs), and they could be stubborn. I'd describe Kayla as stoic, but she endeared herself by obligingly jumping onto the grooming table when asked, sparing me an aching sore back from trying to lift her eighty pounds. After that, I didn't mind grooming her.

One afternoon I stopped at a neighborhood deli for a corned beef Reuben sandwich. There, taped to the door frame, was a large notice:

LOST DOG!!
PART WOLF, PART HUSKY
ANSWERS TO "KAYLA"
REWARD!

I was dismayed. How many wolf-dogs named Kayla could there be in one rural neighborhood? I was certain it was my Kayla, and a concerned phone call to Mr. Marshall confirmed it. Her appearance was that of a purebred wolf—a predator. Someone in the area was bound to shoot her, especially since she was raised as a pet, unafraid of humans, and wouldn't run from them.

Much to my surprise, I received a call from Mr. Marshall a few weeks later. "Jan, Kayla's back! Can you come out right away and give her a bath? She's really stinky."

"Wonderful! Sure will. What's the story on finding her?"

"She just showed up at the back door. We have no clue as to how she survived or what she ate, but she's home. She's happy, we're happy, and Brownie has stopped pouting."

I was as delighted as Mr. Marshall and I continued grooming Kayla for many years after that.

My second encounter with a wolf mixed breed was Dr. Samuelson's wolf-German shepherd. The doctor was a local radio personality who regaled his listeners with tales of his pet, Monty. If you lived in Baltimore, you heard Monty stories. As the dog aged he experienced hip dysplasia resulting in unsteady rear legs. Dr. Samuelson thought it would be less stressful for his twenty-five-year-old dog to be groomed in a mobile unit.

Monty was a wonderful dog, but since he had difficulty standing, I would meet the groomer at Dr. Samuelson's home to help out. The doctor, too, was a generous tipper and paid the charge for two groomers to take care of Monty. We groomed him for five years until he passed away. And again, every visit was a pleasant experience

Because of those previous uneventful wolf encounters, I was nonchalant when a call came in one day to groom a wolf mix. To the usual questions about temperament, Mr. Green replied that his wolf-dog, Killer, was up-to-date on rabies shots and was a good, gentle dog. He agreed to help if needed. Even though we groomed many small and large pooches named "Killer," in retrospect, his name should have raised one of those "Bad Dog Alert" flags, but I let it slide in an attempt to be open-minded.

Joy, a recent graduate from the same grooming school I attended, had responded to our ad in the paper, and I invited her to ride along. A hot prospect, she had a bubbly personality.

I said, "Joy, we're going to be grooming a rather unusual mixed-breed today. He's part wolf and part dog."

"Oh, could that be dangerous?"

"Probably not. We've groomed a few of these kinds of dogs. His owner said he was a good dog." And using my most persuasive voice,

"We should have a fun time." I had high hopes the day would be a good one and she'd jump at the chance to join our small company.

We pulled up to a shabby, uncared-for house, matching its neighborhood. I spotted the wolf-dog patrolling along the higher-than-normal chain link fence in the backyard. Pacing from corner to corner, he had worn a path along its perimeter. He looked like a caged, wild animal at a zoo looking for an escape route.

I cautiously approached the fence. He halted right in front of me. Slowly, turning to face me, he stared into my eyes and growled. His fangs were large and pointed. His coat was a bristly grey. And those feet! They resembled boney falcon talons with sharp untrimmed nails that were curling under and piercing his foot pads. There was nothing cute or adorable about those. He appeared to be pure wolf with distinctive yellow, almond-shaped eyes. What happened to the dog genes?

Killer's owner, Mr. Green, holding a leash in one hand and a large worn muzzle in the other, strolled out to meet me. "Howdy," he said.

As adrenalin raced through me, goosebumps rose on my arms and I tried to stay professional and calm. "What type of dog is your wolf mixed with?"

"Well, we don't rightly know. People down the street, they moved, and we took him," he volunteered.

From his pocket he pulled out a torn, yellowed rabies certificate. I checked the date, praying the inoculation had expired so I could gracefully back out of the commitment. No such luck! Killer's rabies shot was current. Mr. Green dug in his pocket again and removed a pair of leather gloves. He cautiously approached the wolf (notice I've abandoned the "dog" in "wolf-dog"), and after tossing a chunk of raw liver to the animal, he managed to secure a thick leather muzzle over the wolf's jaws.

I watched this exhibition, chills running along my shoulders, heart beating fiercely. This was the so-called gentle animal? Muzzle? This wolf needed more than a muzzle! How about a steel straightjacket?

How about one for me? Had I lost my mind? I should have said, "I'm afraid we won't be able to groom your pet," jumped in the van, floored the gas and shot out of there.

But Joy was waiting to be impressed with how easy and fun it was to groom in a mobile unit. Unwilling to admit defeat and incur the loss of income, I forged ahead and told Mr. Green, "To be on the safe side, why don't you take your pet to the van and place him on the grooming table? I think he'll be more at ease." Yeah, him *and* me.

We were three humans plus one very large, skittish wolf in a tiny 4x6 space. Sweat trickled down my back and into my pants. Joy, on the other hand, appeared unperturbed. She crossed her arms and lounged comfortably against the rear tub, ready to observe this wolf grooming procedure. She probably figured she was with a professional who knew what she was doing.

Mr. Green had a firm grip on Killer's lead, waiting for me to do my thing. Killer, with prominent teeth and lips pulled back but still muzzled, was also waiting. A low snarl escaped from his throat and a ridge of his hair stood up on the middle of his back. Mine stood up on the back of my neck. Again, my instinct was to get the heck out of there and forget about showing off to Joy.

I tried to stall. "Mr. Green, has your dog been groomed before?"

"Well, I took him to a shop, but they couldn't get him out of the cage, even with a muzzle, so don't rightly know just how good he be, but he pretty good 'roun' me."

The words "muzzle" and "good" didn't belong in the same sentence. With my heart beating a mile a minute, I realized that I was the first groomer to deal with Killer. Mentally running through my options, I decided the safest method was to brush out some hair near his rear, as far from those teeth as possible—and see how he responded.

I turned to my job applicant and said in my "instructor" voice, "Joy, in a case like this, I approach the dog from the rear and get him used to my touch. Why don't you stand in back of me?"

To Killer's owner I said, "Mr. Green, I'd like you to get a firm hold on his head."

No longer blasé, Joy quickly moved behind me. At this point, she wanted to take flight from that van as much as I did.

I tentatively brought the brush up to Killer's hindquarters. As soon as it touched him, he went ballistic. He broke the owner's grip, whirled around, opened his jaws, and burst through the muzzle as though it were a shoestring. He snapped at my hand and chomped down.

All three humans screamed. I was certain my hand was amputated. Dazed, I checked it. How could it still be attached to my wrist without even a scratch?

Mr. Green's and Joy's glances followed the brush's flight to the floor where it skittered across in two neatly severed sections. No detached fingers in sight, we all exhaled at the same time.

No way was I going to touch Killer again. He was the alpha wolf, and the three of us, his pack—a tad unhappy pack, I might add—didn't want anything to do with him.

I hoped to, at the minimum, collect a service fee and somehow salvage something from this horrible experience to sustain Joy's interest in joining our firm.

"Mr. Green, Killer is too dangerous to work with. If you'd like, you can use my equipment to brush him out and bathe him yourself. But, I'll have to charge for our time.

Mr. Green decided he didn't want to play any part with this procedure either. Tugging at Killer's leash, he pulled him off the grooming table and paid the service charge. He gave both of us a healthy tip and dragged Killer back to the yard. I figured Killer was going to live out his days without grooming, unless his owner had a vet anesthetize him first.

Shaken, Joy and I sat on the van's front seats, popped open cans of soda and tried to calm our jangled nerves. We sat in silence for ten minutes reliving the incident.

At last Joy turned to me and said, "I thought he had snapped your hand in two. I expected to see a bloody pulp at the end of your wrist! I was so relieved to see the brush on the floor instead of your fingers."

"Me, too! Let's get lunch. My treat."

I checked to make sure Mr. Green's tip would cover a restaurant tab at least one level up from a fast food place. Both of us needed a break before facing another animal. We sat in a booth not saying much. Midway through our feast, Joy looked up and giggled. I put my fork down and burst out laughing.

"Did you see those eyes?" she asked in between bites and snickers. And off we'd go again with snorts and peals of laughter.

I figured I had lost any chance of Joy becoming our newest employee, but apparently my close call served as a bonding experience. She became one of our most talented groomers and stayed with us for years. Her calm demeanor in the van that day was repeated in future difficult situations with clients and pets alike. Every so often, one of us retold the wolf story and our audience chuckled, but it wasn't so funny at the time.

My groomers and I decided that there was an abundance of dirty dogs out there to scratch and bite the hand that grooms them. Why ask for additional problems? As far as scheduling any future mixed breeds, we all agreed the new policy would be: No More Wolves.

Killer was one wolf too many.

16

Those Great
and Wonderful Dogs

. . . .

For the most part, the dogs—and even the cats—I worked with were cooperative. True, the majority of them weren't thrilled when I showed up, but once they were in the van, the grooming generally went well and we were friends afterwards.

However, similar to when I taught second graders and retained more vivid memories of the "difficult" children than the delightful ones in my classroom, so it was with Canine Clippers' clientele. It was easier to recall the dogs that caused a ruckus or had a nasty streak, or the situations in which I made mistakes or had differences of opinion with their cantankerous owners.

But I did groom some outstanding pets. They and their owners stuck in my mind, and it's time I told you about the most memorable of the bunch.

When I first began to groom, I really didn't know much about the different breeds. Yes, I had to memorize what they looked like and had a manual that illustrated how to groom them. Yet, I had no idea how often they required regular grooming or what their typical personalities were like.

Take poodles. What little knowledge I had of them was based on a few TV dog shows. I thought they were too prissy when high-stepping it around the arena. They sported outrageous goofy haircuts with poufs of hair sticking out here and there. I had no interest in a pampered breed for which owners purchased funky hats and clothing to match their own.

Remember Tanya, my "favorite," no-nonsense instructor at grooming school? She set me straight. "Now, poodles basically have nice personalities and are easy to groom," she said. "It's rare for them to be aggressive. They want to please and they're one of the most intelligent breeds. Because you see them every four to six weeks, they'll become your bread and butter."

I thought about my grooming manual and the many different clips for poodles. I asked, "Are we going to have to learn all those different styles?"

She sniffed and said, "Yes, you are. And you're going to have to pass a practical test on every single one. But you probably will never have to memorize more than one or two when you're out there doing your stuff."

"Why's that?"

"Almost all the poodles you'll see will be pets, not show dogs. Don't be thinking a breeder is going to chance you working on one of his blue-ribbon animals. What you'll see are poodles that have little relationship to the standard. You'll find your major job will be to disguise their faults and do the best you can to make them look something like a poodle that their owner will 'ooh' and 'ahh' over."

Tanya was right. It didn't take more than a few months to discover they figured more prominently in our appointment book than any other breed. Take Mrs. Abrams' toy poodle, Carlie.

Grooming Carlie was always a treat. She was one of the few dogs that didn't view my van as a torture chamber and slink away to hide when I arrived. As soon as I pulled up, I heard her frantic barking and joyous whimpering, and I could see her through the picture window running back and forth along the top of the sofa. At each end, she'd stop, look out the window at my progress and howl. After years of Carlie sprinting along the top of Mrs. Abrams' sofa, the fabric had worn down so that only frayed white stuffing showed.

Normally, that sort of behavior was saved for the hated mailman, hoping to scare him away (a successful maneuver—the postman always left), but in this case it meant, "I can hardly wait until you come in to play; did you bring any treats today? Huh? Huh? Hurry up, hurry up!"

Of course, I always carried a few Snausages (doggie treats shaped like pigs in a blanket) in the van. Carlie was tickled to see me, and I was equally happy to see her.

However, the fun was just beginning. First, Carlie played "catch me if you can" around the dining room table, and it was up to me to capture her. Mrs. Abrams, an obese lady, was confined to a wheelchair, and I think racing around the house was the only exercise Carlie ever got.

When I finally coerced her into the van, it was time to play tug-of-war with the leash, and "shake water over the groomer." Her final game was, "see if I can swallow the air from the dryer." She was one wound-up, exuberant pup.

I always took Carlie for a walk (or rather—a romp) after her grooming before returning her to her home. When I tried to leave, she would jump on me and bark. She nipped at my heels until Mrs. Abrams finally picked her up and held her so I could get out the door. What fun to groom a high-spirited dog like Carlie...or an aristocrat like Chanel.

Ruth (we were on a first name basis) wanted only me to groom her show-quality, white standard poodle, Chanel. Ruth and her husband were childless and lived in the suburbs with a two-acre lot kept up according to the regal standards of the neighborhood by a troop of gardeners. Chanel was the queen of the realm. It was a beautiful setting in which to park my van and do the work I loved.

Ruth was the perfect dog owner. Nothing was too good for her Chanel and that filtered down to me as her groomer.

"Now, Jan, you phone me when you're about twenty minutes away and I'll have lunch ready when you arrive." And she did—always serving a Greek delicacy.

As soon as I pulled into her driveway, I heard Chanel announce my presence with one, and only one, bark. Any more would be undignified.

Standing tall and stoic, she met me at the door and allowed me to scratch behind her ears. She patiently waited until after lunch before standing at the door with the leash in her mouth as if to say, "It's about time now to give me a little attention."

After I finished Ruth's gourmet lunch, I walked Chanel to the van. Smart and cooperative, she jumped inside and onto the grooming table with a smidgen of encouragement from me. Then she'd watch me with her beautiful, dark, long-lashed, brown eyes, while politely withstanding the hours of brushing, prodding, pulling—all the grooming a standard poodle needs before bathing. After that, it was a good hour of drying, brushing, drying, brushing, and on and on. Never once did the queen show she objected by snapping or lying down.

One time she jumped out of the van before I was ready to walk her back to her palace, but she simply gave me a look that said, "It's all good baby. No need to stress yourself," and waited for me to climb out and accompany her.

I looked forward to seeing both Ruth and Chanel, and I think they enjoyed my visits, too. To top it off—and I almost hate to mention it—Ruth not only fed me, but her check included a very generous tip. Frankly, I would have groomed Chanel for nothing just to be a member of her court.

Groomers loved the big dogs. Most were gentle giants, seldom aggressive and delighted with any attention. Many were short-coated, and a quick brushing out to loosen up dead hair, trimming of nails, cleaning of ears and a bath completed their grooming needs. They were what we called, "easy money." But the characteristic that most endeared them to us was their friendliness.

Yet after several groomers, including me, injured our backs and were put out of commission for over a week, we changed our policy to scheduling only dogs weighing less than fifty pounds. Unfortunately, the new guidelines meant we had to give up the many good-natured larger breeds—the retrievers, the setters, the collies, and most sadly, the wonderful standard poodles (except Chanel; I had to keep my favorite!).

While owning Canine Clippers, I made it a point to watch the Westminster and Eukanuba dog shows each year. Whichever breed won "Best in Show" was certain to become extremely popular, and we groomers would see them for years.

Niel would hear me complain, "Darn! Look at that. A cocker won."

"Isn't that good? Don't you want a dog with 'hair' to win? I mean, it doesn't help if a Rottweiler wins. How many of their owners have called for an appointment?"

But I knew what I was in for. With cocker spaniels, I could expect the unexpected. Like Kris' dog, Snookers, they had unpredictable personalities. Some were schizophrenic. One minute you were their friend, the next their enemy, and so I was wary. Others were sweet and loving—and like Taffy, I smiled when I found they were scheduled on my route.

Taffy's owners, the Kellers, didn't have the funds to have her groomed more than every three or four months. But, like many other older folks, their kids were long gone, and Taffy was like a child to them. I was aware that they saved up until they could afford to have her groomed. But because I saw her so infrequently, I usually had to shave off most of her matted fur.

True to her breed's trait of urinating when anyone (and I mean anyone—including her family...*especially* her family) arrived at her door, Taffy favored me with that welcome every time. I never figured out what that was all about, but after picking her up, I usually ended up as wet and stinky as the mat by her front door.

But then she patiently stood on the table, scarcely moving as I inched the clippers very carefully through her thick matted hair. Now and then she'd turn to look at me as if to ask, "Aren't we done yet?" She'd put her nose to my nose and give me an Eskimo kiss. She knew exactly when the last hunk of hair came off, and that's when she pranced around on the table, as excited as I was that we were almost finished.

Taffy sprang from the grooming table, across a cabinet, and into the tub. I removed my wet, smelly smock and threw it in after her. I sprayed her and my smock with water, shampooed both and rinsed them. For my final act, I hung up my smock and aimed the dryer both at it and Taffy.

She bounced back to her home. She seemed to know that all her dirty hair was gone. She was looking oh-so-good and better yet, we both smelled fresh as a Tide washed load of laundry—at least for the moment.

Mrs. Keller thought so, too. She rewarded Taffy with a doggie treat and me with an iced tea. I learned to schedule Taffy over lunchtime as Mrs. Keller insisted I stay for a bite to eat (the baloney sandwich was my tip and I never minded). I looked forward to Taffy's appointments, and I made it a point to take two smocks with me on those days.

May, a single, middle-aged woman, lived in Federal Hill—one of the oldest but well preserved historical, downtown neighborhoods in Baltimore. One morning when she opened her door, she found a dog on her doorstep huddled next to *The Baltimore Sun*. A dog lover, she invited the basset hound/American bulldog mix in for food and drink. After slurping up his breakfast, he scratched at her front door and she let him out.

Throwing on a coat, May followed him up the street and around the corner. He waddled into an open service garage and settled himself near the door.

May asked a repairman, "Does that dog live here?"

"No, ma'am," he said, "Montgomery just comes here every day to work."

"Work! What does he do?"

"Well, nothing, really, he just comes here every morning and hangs out with the guys—I'd say he's sort of an overseer."

"Do you know where he lives or where he goes every evening?"

"Nope, don't know. He just shows up mornings—has for years."

"How'd he get his name?"

"We've always called him that."

May returned home and drove to work. That evening when she returned, the dog was, again, sitting on her doorstep.

"Well, Montgomery, are you hungry? Want to come in?"

Montgomery sauntered inside and went directly to May's kitchen where the food and water dishes from that morning still sat. May fed him and he spent the night. The next morning, when May left for work, so did Montgomery. He was one serious worker, always punctual and never asking for a day off.

Montgomery had apparently been living on the streets for some time and May decided he had adopted her. She phoned us to clean him up. By then, she had already taken him to a vet and he was up-to-date on his rabies shots. He appeared healthy, but was one funky dog. His skin was scarred and scabby with white patches, as though it had been burned. There was also a mysterious odor about him that I couldn't quite place. I bathed him with a medicated shampoo, but within a week May phoned.

"Jan, Montgomery smells again, how soon can you come over?"

I had picked up my van from Mike's auto repair shop that morning, and when I arrived and took a whiff of Montgomery, a light bulb went on. I recognized that odor. I had just left it at Mike's shop. Montgomery smelled of oil and tires, like the rest of his garage crew.

I continued grooming him for many years, and May always expressed how grateful she was that Montgomery had chosen her. I figured it was no coincidence that May's two-century-old home was located on Montgomery Street.

There were two breeds that were not that well known when I started my business, but the longer I groomed, the more popular they became. One was the bichon frise, a little powder puff of a dog with a plumed tail carried jauntily over its back. These dogs were so smart that they were often used in circuses to perform tricks. Because the breed was a novelty in the U.S. (although descended from 13th-century Spanish water spaniels), many owners didn't realize they had a high-maintenance dog on their hands.

The year a bichon won the Westminster, I knew we were in for it. They were one of the few dogs that did not shed, but whose coats grew longer and longer. Many owners had no clue that if they didn't brush them out daily, their double-coat fur would become hopelessly matted. On the up side, like poodles, they became the groomer's newest bread and butter.

Muffin (confirmed by a computer search as the most popular name for small dogs) was friendly and outgoing, just like her energetic mistress, Amanda. The two lived in one of the Inner Harbor's renovated row houses, and other than having to deal with the tricky parking situation in those neighborhoods, I enjoyed seeing them. Amanda was religious about caring for Muffin and not only brushed her daily, but scheduled monthly appointments. I was proud that she looked the way a fluffy bichon should, and that I didn't have to scalp her like so many others.

An artist and poet, Amanda assumed the casual fashion in her Soho-style Baltimore neighborhood. Funky dress was the uniform, and if your hair was as straight as a plank and you wore ethnic jewelry, you fit in beautifully. As time went on, I didn't even notice street people with bright green or purple hair and fringed Native-American clothing (worn by palefaces). Coffeehouses and secondhand boutiques, rather than grocery and hardware stores, were strung along the streets.

Although casual about everything else, Amanda was exacting when it came to Muffin's grooming and critiqued my clip after I brought her back in. I learned to tuck a comb and scissors in my pocket and for the next half hour, snip a hair here and there as she spotted a strand just an eighth of an inch higher than the one next to it. I did more trimming inside her home than in the van!

One day after grooming Muffin, I came out and found a ticket on my window. I had overstayed my two-hour parking limit. I decided to invite Amanda into the van for the next grooming and save some precious minutes. It worked out well. While I made Muffin gorgeous, Amanda read Edgar Allan Poe tales and poems to me, and every so often looked up and said, "You see that piece there on her leg, could you just trim that a bit closer?"

To this day I can recite "The Raven" from memory.

The second "new" breed America latched onto was the Portuguese water dog (or PWD). Its pedigree was quite old, going back to when its medieval ancestors helped Portuguese fishermen herd fish into nets. They became so popular that President Obama accepted Senator Kennedy's gift of one for his family. (I e-mailed the White House suggesting they rethink their choice. I figured they wouldn't have a problem keeping their new pet in tip-top shape while he was president, but what about after, when the girls were in charge of brushing this high-maintenance animal? I didn't receive a response.)

Chad, prior to the establishment of our fifty pound weight limit, was the first PWD that I groomed. He was so tall that the top of his head brushed the ceiling of the van. There were several different accepted clips for PWDs, but most owners wanted the retriever clip, which left about one inch of hair all over and a tuft at the end of the curling tail.

I had allotted two hours for his grooming, and was appalled when I got him in the van and looked him over. I didn't know where to begin. His seemingly boundless, rough black coat was about six inches long. If I didn't get rid of that hair first, I would be there all day brushing, not to mention the drying time after his bath. At that moment I wished for the luxury of working in a salon shop where I could do a little work and take a break before plunging in again. But in a mobile van, Chad was a start-to-finish and no-rest-for-the-weary customer.

My executive decision-making was taking a wee bit too long, and Chad sat down on his haunches. I knew he was thinking, "Are we ever going to get started with this?"

I finally settled on scissoring off five inches of hair to leave the one inch I wanted. Still, it took three hours to brush, clip, bathe and trim Chad. But the time flew by as he and I talked to one another. Whatever I asked him to do—turn around, sit, give me his paw—he did and nuzzled me as though to say, "Anything you need, I'm good for it."

Chad was a dream dog—a veritable saint—until it was time for his bath. Then all hell broke loose and he fought the water like the devil.

I struggled to shove all of his sixty-five pounds into the tub, and then had to wrestle to keep him there. Once we were done, however, Chad reverted to his easygoing, gentlemanly self, and I wondered, "How come this PWD, whose ancestors were bred to work in water, had such an aversion to it?"

An added benefit to grooming Chad was parking my van in the bucolic countryside under the lovely oak trees growing near the Newmans' driveway. What a joy—a level spot, shade and a great dog. It was all good (except for that bath business).

I charged Mrs. Newman sixty dollars and felt I should have upped the price, but I was ignorant of the amount of work and time involved in grooming a PWD and had low-balled my over-the-phone estimate.

She, on the other hand, was outraged. "Jan, I think that's way too much. Chad's only a dog. I don't pay that much to have my own hair done!"

Both of us were disgruntled.

I should have asked her to consider that if she grew dreadlocks for a couple of months, what her hairdresser would charge. Plus, I would bet that Mrs. Newman's hairdresser never had to worry about getting bit when her customers got tired of her pulling and tugging on their hair.   I was more than upset that Mrs. Newman, with her designer clothes, custom-made earrings, and castle of a house, haggled over her expensive $3,000 dog's sixty dollar grooming.

The lesson for me was: If a dog was not in the best of shape and I would have to up the price, I invited the owner into the van. A frank discussion about the relationship between time and money took place before the owner or I became upset.

Interestingly, when Mrs. Newman took Chad to a pet salon the next time, she was charged $125. After that, she scheduled appointments with Canine Clippers.

Much to my surprise, before we adjusted our policy to scheduling only dogs weighing less than fifty pounds, we groomed more large, short-haired dogs than I had anticipated. Since they didn't require regular bathing, I wondered why so many owners insisted on professional grooming. I decided it was because owners were generally anxious about clipping their dogs' nails. Once they misjudged where the vein ended and drew blood, it was all over and they called us.

Canine Clippers groomed several long-legged greyhounds whose heads brushed the van ceiling. They were generally racetrack dogs that had been rescued after their careers ended, and they were a tad skittish about everything, including stairs. Knowing very little about race dogs, one owner enlightened me when she explained, "Jan, they're kept in large kennels between races and probably have never been near a set of stairs. I had to train mine to climb them when we first adopted him."

That's why it took two people to get one jittery greyhound into the van. But they were very sweet animals to bathe once they were in the tub. They seemed to relish any affection bestowed on them. I also learned that they were thin-skinned, and groomers needed to be cautious when using products, such as flea dips, that could harm them. Their owners were well aware of their pets' limitations and were quick to inform groomers of them. Thank God for rescue organizations!

We worked with Doberman pinschers and Rottweilers, usually muzzling them at the start, at least until we became familiar with a particular dog. They were, after all, bred to be guard dogs, but most of them were okay. Pit bulls, on the other hand...

I was nervous driving to my first appointment with one. I had never groomed a Staffordshire bull terrier (the proper name for a pit bull) in school, and although its owner, Mrs. Patrick, said Chip had been groomed many times and without incident, I was sorry I had scheduled him on my own route. The word on the street was that they could turn on you, and the media was saturated with stories of confrontations between pit bulls and humans. The humans generally were on the losing end.

When I arrived, Mrs. Patrick showed me Chip's rabies certificate, led him to the van and helped me lift him onto the table.

"You be a good boy," she said and left.

"Oooh, wait a minute," I thought, "wouldn't you like to stick around a bit, just in case?"

Chip looked at me, I looked at him. His teeth and strong jaws, perfectly designed to grip and hang on to his target, were so dangerous, so intimidating. The seconds lasted forever while we stared at each other. Chip made the first move. He abruptly swung his head within inches of mine. I jerked back, but not in time to avoid his rough, wet tongue.

"Oh," I whispered, "Oh, what a loving dog."

And he was, indeed. So were all the rest of the pit bulls we were privileged to groom.

Did it surprise you to find pit bulls in this chapter on wonderful dogs? Were you thinking they belonged in "Horror 'Tails'"? You were wrong and so was I, until I learned never to judge a dog by the breed's reputation, but as individual dogs with their own personalities.

It took me some time to discover that many of them proved they belonged right here in "Those Great and Wonderful Dogs."

17
Future Groomers of America

Because running Canine Clippers consumed most of my days and many of my evenings, my main recreation was Sunday morning church. But there were a few rare occasions when I tried to escape for a different kind of fun.

In the early days, when an invitation arrived for a party, I was itching to go in anticipation of good food and conversation *not* revolving around dogs—the economy, the government, the Ravens. But it seldom worked out. As soon as other guests discovered I was the resident "pet expert," I never made it to the buffet. After dealing with them day after day, I soon discovered that unless I arrived incognito (doctors and lawyers have mastered this art), that option wasn't open to me.

Actually, I didn't mind giving out free advice—I loved my job and cared about the animals. So I treasured those times when I "planned" to be the center of attention, especially when I could teach children how to care for their pets and tell them about my career.

Mrs. Keller, one of Canine Clippers' clients and an enthusiastic PTA booster, asked me to participate in "Truck Day" at her daughter's preschool.

She explained, "We invite all types of businesses that use trucks. They park them at the school and talk about what they do with them. I'd love to have you come and demonstrate how you groom pets in your van. Would you consider that?"

"I sure would. Tell me how it works."

"The children will be divided into groups of about eight or so. A teacher and parent chaperone them as they walk from truck to truck. I think of it as a career day for toddlers."

"I'd love to do that, Mrs. Keller," I said, "but I'd need access to electricity so my clippers and dryer will be available. But, I don't want the children tripping over the extension cord."

"Tell you what," she said, mulling over my concern, "how about placing your van close to an outlet on the school's outside wall and that way the cord won't be in their path?"

When I suggested that the little ones might find it interesting to watch me handle a dog, Mrs. Keller volunteered to bring her mixed breed, short-haired Howie. She said she'd convince a couple of friends to bring their dogs, too. I didn't think any more about it, other than to make sure a van was free for the day.

Mrs. Keller phoned a few days before the big event. "Jan, Carol's going to bring her Pekingese, and Hannah has a cocker spaniel that's very good around children."

I decided I would groom Howie first. He loved his bath, and I'd show the children how dogs were bathed in the van. The other two I'd just brush out, demonstrate my clipper shaving off belly hair, maybe clean their ears and clip a couple of nails. I intended to enjoy my day off the road.

As I pulled into the school parking lot, I saw a garbage truck, a tow truck, and a truck loaded with thousands of gallons of pool water parked there already. An oil tanker pulled in behind me, followed by a furniture mover. I stopped next to a guy with an orange vest directing drivers, and he waved me to the middle of the parking lot.

Whoa! I rolled down my window, hung my head out and shouted, "No, I'm supposed to be next to the school!"

He checked his chart. "Nope, says here Canine Clippers is between the fire truck and the ambulance."

No electricity! I was stumped. Should I just turn around and go home, or perhaps, pull over and see if I could locate Mrs. Keller?

The oil tanker's driver decided for me when he honked and yelled, "Canine Clippers, you moving or what? That rig behind me is hanging out into traffic."

I found my spot between the fire truck and ambulance. The emergency vehicle and I were two little vans towered over by huge eighteen-wheelers—the circus dwarfs between two giants at a midway show.

Most of the truck drivers were milling around. The ambulance guy joked, "Hey, Canine Clippers, if you injure a dog, I'm right here—wouldn't be the first time I rushed a dog to a vet." Very funny.

It was almost 1 p.m., starting time, and I could see groups of small children lined up at the school's rear glass doors. I decided to forget about electricity and make the most of the situation. The day was getting quite warm, and I wouldn't dry any of the dogs. My lights, my water pump and my water heater would work off the battery—if I ran the van every so often. I checked my gas gauge—yep, my fuel was OK.

Mrs. Keller, looking official holding her clipboard and dressed in a snappy red blazer, arrived with Howie in tow. "All the children will be wearing name tags," she said, adding with a little smile, "Of course, you don't get one since they can't read."

She noticed I wasn't amused—no smile on my face. "Everything okay with you, Jan?"

"Well, I've got a little problem. I thought you were going to place me next to the school with access to electricity."

"Oh, right. Well, I was told that wouldn't work out. The Library Bookmobile needed to park there," she offered matter-of-factly. She pleaded, "Can't you do everything right where you are? We don't want to disappoint the children, do we?"

"I can manage, but I won't be able to dry the dogs or use my electric clipper."

"Oh, that won't matter. The main thing is to show the children the van."

So much for the children's "interest" watching my demonstration.

When the chaperones brought the first group, the little tykes immediately wanted to climb into my van. That wasn't going to work. If I had been apprehensive about a little electrical cord tripping them up, I sure didn't want them in the van with a dog. I asked the attending adults to make sure the children just looked through the door.

The preschoolers laughed and giggled as I showed them how to brush a dog and clean its ears. Everyone wanted to pet Howie, and knowing his temperament, I sat in the doorway and allowed them. Howie loved it and so did I.

I placed him in the bathtub and they craned their necks to watch me bathe him. Howie was soaped up and ready for his rinse when a tot asked, "Mrs. Groomer, does that dog bite?"

I glanced at her name tag. "No, Jessica, his name is Howie, and he's a very good dog."

Their ten minutes at my location over, the next group of preschoolers arrived. I recognized Mrs. Keller's daughter and said, 'Hi, Stacy, Howie's being very good today."

She turned to her classmates, and I heard the pride in her voice when she said, "That's my dog. His name is Howie."

The split second Howie recognized Stacy's voice, he attempted to scramble out of the tub. I grabbed him, but he was still soapy and slipped right through my hands to the floor. He slid across it and out the door to Stacy.

Standing next to her was a small red-haired, Orphan Annie look-alike, and Howie sensed she needed to be greeted, too. He jumped on her and decided this was the perfect time to shake off those suds.

She ducked and bawled, "I'm wet. I want my mama." She broke away from the group and, trailed by her teacher, ran to the double glass doors.

By then, Howie had rubbed up against another child who yelled, "Mrs. Groomer, Mrs. Groomer, that dog's got soap all over me."

The parent chaperone decided that was enough excitement for her charges and led them over to the fire engine. I jumped down, looped a leash over Howie's head and lifted him back into the van. After plopping him into the tub and rinsing off the shampoo, I dried him with a towel.

The sun was now high in the sky, and my van doubled as a sauna. I wondered if the fireman was going to demonstrate the fire hose and really get the kids soaked. I wouldn't have minded a couple of jet sprays myself!

Mrs. Keller moseyed over to collect Howie, and right behind her was her friend, Carol, with her Pekingese.

I explained, "Thank you for bringing your dog. I'm sorry to tell you that I don't have electricity and I can't dry him."

"Oh, that's OK," she said placidly. Mingo can just air dry."

Relieved to have a laid-back, "anything goes" owner, I had her bring Mingo into the van and within a blink, another cluster of children marched my way. I abandoned the sweltering interior to simply sit in the doorway. Mingo was very patient as I held him and talked to the children about dogs and how I cleaned them.

That group left, and while I waited for a third, I thought this was a good moment to begin brushing Mingo. I reached for the brush and his eyes followed my hand. As soon as I touched it, he growled.

Uh-oh, I hadn't expected that reaction. Was he psychic, or did he recognize the brush? I said, "Are you going to be a good boy?"

Mingo raised his upper lip and showed me his gums and teeth.

Guess not.

What to do? The next group was at the van door ready to hear what I had to say.

I smiled and, turning Mingo's hostility into a teaching opportunity, said, "Well, children, not every dog likes to be groomed. I think this one might be one of them."

Mingo's owner hadn't gone too far away and rushed over when she heard her dog growling.

I asked her, "Ah, I'm having some problems with Mingo; has he been groomed before?"

"Well, actually, they usually have to muzzle him, but I figured you had one in the van and knew how to deal with a dog like him."

Sure I did. But I didn't think a muzzling exhibition would go over big with my audience. What was she thinking to bring a dog like that around small children? I said, "Perhaps it's best for you to take him back."

Carol gave me a dirty look. "I was thinking of scheduling an appointment with you to groom Mingo, but if you don't know how to handle him, forget it." She snatched him from my arms and stomped off.

Maybe she wasn't so laid-back after all.

I had about half an hour until the cocker spaniel was due. I wasn't very happy with this situation, although the kids were really sweet and attentive. Lots of laughing and pointing to various tools and asking, "What's that, Mrs. Groomer?"

I spritzed a bit of cologne their way, "That's to make the dogs smell good."

One precocious youngster piped up, "My dog farts a lot. He never smells good. Would that stuff work?"

"Ah, no. Probably not, Matt. Does anyone else have a question?"

Mrs. Keller strolled over and said, "Hannah just called. Her dog ran off when he saw the leash. So, I guess you lost your last dog."

Great! I was fine with that and just enjoyed being with the children. I even allowed a few to come in and look around the van.

It would have been a great day, except that when I was ready to leave, my van wouldn't start. But, lucky me, the "Truck Day" tow truck driver recognized a damsel in distress and hauled my van down to Mike's Auto Repair.

As much as I enjoyed the preschoolers, I had a hunch that older children would be a better age group to learn about pet care. Therefore, when several months later, Mrs. Evans, the principal at one of Baltimore's elementary schools, asked me to speak to the fourth grade class, I was more than happy to accept.

"Are the children going to be able to come outside so I can show them the van?" I asked.

"No. I don't think that would be a good idea. Security, you know."

Well, no, I didn't really know. Half the fun was showing off my unusual van, but I figured I'd bring my dog, Ginger, for added interest.

I drove into the city on the scheduled day, found the school and tried to locate a gate in the chain-link fence around its perimeter. Canine Clippers groomed many dogs in the area, and while it was in a poorer section of town, I didn't consider it dangerous. I guessed they weren't taking any chances. Fortunately, we now had cell phones, and I used mine to dial the school.

"Is the principal, Mrs. Evans, there? This is Jan Nieman. I'm here to give a demonstration to a fourth grade class. I'm parked on the street and can't locate the entrance to the school grounds."

The secretary said, "OK, I'll have our janitor open up for you. Drive around to the rear."

After he unlocked the gate and showed me where to park, I grabbed my grooming case, and with Ginger on a leash, entered the school.

My tiny pup must have looked like a charging lion to the student wandering in the hallway. She hugged the wall, pointed at Ginger and screamed at a decibel usually reserved for the playground, "There's a dog in the school! There's A DOG in here!"

I smiled and attempted to calm her. "Yes, this is Ginger, she's going to go with me to the fourth grade classroom."

It didn't matter, she kept shrieking, "…A DOG, A DOG!"

Mrs. Evans poked her head out of her office. "I didn't realize you'd be bringing a dog." She apologized, "I'm sorry. Many of these children are afraid of them. They think all dogs are like the pit bulls in their neighborhoods."

"Well, Ginger is very good and I'll be keeping her on a leash. Do you think it's OK for me to bring her in the classroom?"

I heard the reluctance in her voice when she said, "I suppose so," and led me to Mrs. Herman's fourth grade room.

As soon as I entered, whatever lesson Mrs. Herman was teaching was drowned out by the uproar of the children when they spotted Ginger. They screamed, laughed, hooted—instant pandemonium. A few hid under their desks. It was as though they'd never seen a dog before. Chaos ruled.

"Children, return to your seats!" Mrs. Herman shouted over the din.

While she attempted to restore decorum to her out-of-control class, I set my tool case and Ginger on a front table.

When the students finally settled back in their seats, I said, "Hi, children, my name is Mrs. Nieman. I'm a dog groomer, and this little dog's name is Ginger. She's a rescue dog. Do you know what that means?"

A boy in the front row leaned over his desk and said, "... you rescued her from the river?"

"No, but that's a very good guess." I went on to tell them the story of how Ginger was rescued from some boys swinging her by her tail.

"Oh, that's awful," a fourth grader in the rear said. "My dad brought home a dog from the bar. He said he rescued it from guzzling beer other men gave it. He still likes beer, though, and walks around in circles. His name is Beer Belly."

Hoping to squelch more unsuitable rescue stories, I said, "How many of you own a dog or kitty?" About five students raised their hands. "What I'd like to share with you today is how to take care of your pet."

I then showed the class a nail clipper and trimmed Ginger's nails. They were spellbound and peppered me with questions. I felt pretty good about the experience.

It was time to go, but before I wrapped up the lesson, I held up two pink bows and asked, "What do you think is the last thing a groomer does before giving the dog back to its owner?"

The same boy in the front row pointed to Ginger. "Clean up the pee?"

I looked down at Ginger. She had, indeed, urinated on the table.

Everyone in the classroom roared and I sensed my fragile control of the audience slipping. I mopped the desk, sprayed it with disinfectant and quickly attached two bows to Ginger's ears. As I packed away my tools, I asked, "What's the most important thing you learned today?"

My quick little friend in the front said, "Always take your dog for a walk before you bring her in."

I clapped my hands and smiled. "You are absolutely right."

And yes, the next time I took Ginger to a school as Exhibit A, we went for a short walk first.

Several years later, long after our five children had attended the school, the career counselor at their high school invited me to participate in "Career Day." I was delighted to be asked. This would be a chance to discuss my vocation with students who might be considering pet grooming.

We "professionals" were seated in the gymnasium at twenty-five tables. Each presenter had ten chairs facing them. Large signs stating our profession were taped to the walls behind us. I checked them out: Doctor, Accountant, Nurse—most of them required further education or a college degree. I felt quite out of place with my blue-collar job and "Pet Groomer" hanging over my head.

The double doors opened and in filed about fifty students. The homeroom teachers sent their students to the gym for a half hour to ask questions or sit in on a mini-presentation. Most looked bored as they glanced at the signs. A few immediately strode over to the "Doctor," several walked toward the "Teacher," and then I saw her.

A sullen student with unkempt hair, not quite making the latest high-school fashion statement, spotted the sign over my head. She poked a classmate with her elbow and nodded in my direction. I guessed they were snickering that anyone would consider pet grooming. To my surprise, she and her friend headed my way and parked themselves in two chairs.

OK, at least I had a couple of students sitting with me. But then several more approached and within a few seconds all ten chairs were filled—mostly with girls.

Wow, was it possible I had ten future groomers of America gathered around me? My concern about being out-of-place vanished, and as I checked out the other presenters, I noticed half their chairs were unoccupied. How about that? I had won the Battle of the Chairs.

The girl who had spotted me first sat directly in front and said, "I wanted to be a vet, but my dad doesn't have the money to send me to vet school. Besides, we found out there wasn't one in Maryland and I'd have to go out of state, so that really put it out of my reach. What's pet grooming?"

"I'm glad you asked that. If someone, like you, loves to work with animals but can't afford to spend six years or more attending a veterinarian school, then this job is perfect for them. You can learn to be a groomer several ways."

I warmed to my subject: "I enrolled in a grooming school, and when I graduated, I had been taught enough to open my own business. If you take that path, you'll spend about twelve weeks in school and it'll cost about the same as one semester at a state college."

The girl frowned and interrupted, "I don't know if my folks could even afford that."

"Many students apprentice at a grooming salon where the owner agrees to train them in exchange for their services at a minimum wage. Taking that route is slower, but on the other hand, you do earn an income along the way."

Although it was obvious from her dress that she wasn't in step with her more affluent classmates, she was earnest and interested. I wished she had a name tag like the preschool youngsters. "What is your name?" I asked her.

"I'm Marcie," she said. For the first time she grinned and nodded to her friend. "I guess grooming could be a possibility."

"Well, Marcie, there is one more way, and that's to purchase a book about grooming and learn from it. But there are two major drawbacks to that. One is finding cats or dogs to practice on. There aren't many owners who want a novice working on their beloved pet. The other is that without guidance from a professional, you really won't be taught how to groom all the different breeds, or pick up advice from other groomers."

I was on a roll and noticed my group of ten had expanded to three more students who had swiped chairs from the "professional" next to me.

"Take trimming dog nails," I said. "Sometimes dogs don't like you clipping their nails, and you have to be tricky about doing it. There are all sorts of dog holds that you'd never think of yourself. Really, the information you receive when you work with other groomers is invaluable."

Marcie now had both elbows on my table and leaned forward. "What can a groomer make?"

"If you work in a shop, you can expect to earn around $30,000 a year, plus tips."

"Wow!" said my gal, Marcie.

"If you own your own shop, you have more expenses, but the more groomers you employ, the more you'll make."

My future groomers whistled and the policeman next to me bent in my direction. He whispered, "What did you just say? How much does a groomer earn?"

I repeated it, and since no one was sitting in front of him he scooted his chair over and joined the kids.

Handing him my business card, I whispered back, "I've hired many second-career folks."

After I finished speaking, I passed out pamphlets I had designed with information about a pet grooming career.

The bell rang, and as my group filed out, Marcie said, "Thank you Mrs. Nieman, I didn't know about grooming. I think I would like that even better than being a vet. I won't have to see dogs in pain, or being brought in after being hit by a car, or even worse, having to put them down."

"You're absolutely right about that. You get to clean them up and love them and make them look and feel wonderful without seeing them hurt. It's all good—and the money isn't bad either, considering it doesn't take four years or more to learn your trade."

The pattern with the students continued during the rest of "Career Day." They walked in, glanced around, and most sat down in front of white-collar professionals. But many of the remaining ones wandered over to me. Unlike being the center of attention at a party, this venue was more fulfilling when I discussed my career.

The bell rang and my last group filed out, but their middle-aged student advisor lingered. She asked me, the equally middle-aged "Pet

Groomer," "Would you be willing to return next year? You certainly were popular."

"I sure would!"

"And if a student wanted more information about becoming a dog groomer, could they contact you?"

"Certainly."

She glanced around, and seeing no other teachers, leaned closer. She lowered her voice and said, "Ah, could I have one of those brochures? I'm thinking I need a career change and this might be just the ticket."

18
Throwing In the Towel

Time flies when you're having fun, and twenty-one years later, we'd had a bit too much and definitely were past retirement age. I could tell because when we showed up at restaurants for the "Early Bird Senior Specials," the hostess didn't ask for our ID. Most of our friends had already sailed into their golden years, and we didn't appear to be on the same boat as far as *living the good life*. They spoke of brunch dates, sleeping in and booking cruises.

My brunch dates were spent with dogs. If a favorite pup happened to be on the grooming table and it was lunchtime, we shared a sand-wich—one bite for me and one bite for the dog.

I didn't recognize the phrase "sleeping in." Hitting the snooze button was not an option when my groomers expected their vans to be ready to roll at 7:30.

Cruises? I cruised all right—circling around and around the Baltimore Beltway. Our vacations typically landed in the week after New Year's Day. At that point all the holiday pets had been groomed, and clients were more concerned with paying for gift purchases than incurring additional expenses. But when we closed for an entire week, no revenue came in to pay the previous week's wages and that presented a miserly vacation for us. We generally drove our elderly motor home to Florida and camped at RV parks.

Our groomers were thrilled with their paid vacations, compliments of the Maryland state unemployment office. None of them objected to the enforced time off, and some sprinted out of town before we did. So much for the claim that owning your own business meant,

"You can keep your own hours and take vacations when you like" or the even more misleading, "Your time is your own and you're your own boss." Don't believe a word of it! My time belonged to my clients and employees. I hoarded my hard-fought-over moments of leisure as though the end of the world were on my doorstep.

I wasn't coping well with the physical and emotional stress of keeping the business afloat. My back and arms ached after a day of grooming. My feet hurt. I was less patient with difficult dogs and found myself raising a brush to bop them on the head instead of gently stroking them with it. At times, when they refused to cooperate, I had to stifle screaming, "Stop that! Behave!" And to top it off, my groomers were taking home a bigger paycheck than I was.

Niel was weary of laundering sixty to seventy towels a day, six days a week. He said, "I thought I gave this up after the five kids were out of diapers." Food shopping, fixing dinner and dealing with a grouchy, sometimes zombie-like wife hadn't been precisely what he bargained for. The thrill of the hunt for replacement parts for our mature (OK, junkyard-ready) vans was long gone.

Obviously, we had held on too long making a go of this semi-successful business. While we had plenty of customers and a troop of excellent groomers, we just couldn't keep our expenses lower than our income. We thought each month would be better, but better never arrived. Still, we needed a shove to bail out.

The day a notice from the Baltimore County zoning board arrived was a blessing in disguise. Seems that after twenty-one years of parking business vans in our driveway, a real estate agent, attempting to sell a neighboring home, filed a complaint. The letter informed us it was illegal to park more than *one* commercial vehicle in a driveway in an area zoned for residential homes. There were *five* of the rusty gems in ours.

That was the final nudge to face reality and call it quits. But now that we had made the decision, we needed some guidance. Where was the help and advice from the Small Business Administration now?

Why didn't they offer seminars called "Exit Strategies"? Where were the manuals on "How to End Your Business" or "Depression Therapy for Those Facing Bankruptcy"? Then again, would one have time to read these helpful books or sit in a class when one is scrambling to survive? As usual, we flew by the seat of our pants, or in my case, by my grooming smock, and brainstormed exit possibilities.

Did you ever wonder where that phrase "throwing in the towel" came from? Here's the scoop: It's boxing lingo. It refers to when a fighter is getting hopelessly pummeled, and his manger literally throws a towel into the ring to end the bout. That was us, all right.

Our first step in throwing in the towel was to sell the business. But when we tried to place a value on the vans, that fantasy crumbled into dust. First, four of them wouldn't pass inspection, and investing thousands of dollars to bring them up to code seemed foolish. If possible buyers peeked into each van's six-inch-thick repair file, they would turn tail and back off before negotiations even began. No, the vans weren't marketable.

What about the customer list, you ask? Wow, when I added them up, 4,500 customers sounded like a lot, and potentially lucrative. But unless some other mobile pet grooming company owned five extra vans, they would find it impossible to service those customers. Selling the client list to our groomers was also out of the question. For years they had traveled to customers' homes. The list existed not only in our computer files, but also in their heads. There really wasn't anything saleable except our good name, and our good name was departing for Florida.

There was also that nagging feeling of responsibility to our staff. My son, Dave, one of Canine Clippers' all-time top groomers, had already gotten fed up with working in the ever-breaking-down vans and taken flight for employment in a brick-and-mortar pet grooming shop. Our five remaining groomers had given us many years of faithful service, and suddenly closing up shop and leaving them high and dry without jobs felt unfair. We didn't relish informing our customers, either.

So we came up with "The Plan."

We advised our groomers that, if they chose, they could rent one of our deteriorating vans for one dollar for one year and assume all insurance and repairs. At the year's end, and when they had purchased a van of their own (hopefully), they were to deliver the vans to the Humane Society of Baltimore County.

Excited, all of them took us up on our offer. It gave them the perfect opportunity to own their own business (apparently they were unaware that I earned less than they did). For the next two months they delivered letters to their customers explaining they would still be available to groom their beloved pets. The letters listed each groomer's new business name and phone number.

At the close of Canine Clippers' final week, we invited our five groomers to select what they wished from our leftover supplies. Each of them picked a number from a basket and in turn chose the items they wanted. Spray paint, water pumps and blow-dryers found their way from our stacked-to-the-ceiling shelves to their growing mini-mounds. Along with the inventory, we threw in two hundred well-laundered, slightly frayed towels.

My mother put in her bid. "Say, those towels make excellent cleaning rags; could you save a dozen for me?"

News of our retirement traveled fast.

Dismayed, Mrs. Ross called, "Jan, I heard you were going out of business. Is this true?"

My voice was peppy and enthusiastic as though this was an extraordinary opportunity for us. "Mrs. Ross, thank you for calling. Yes, it's true! I'm happy to tell you that after twenty-one years of operating Canine Clippers, we are retiring."

"Oh my goodness! Who's going to take care of my Freddy?"

"Here's the good news. Sarah, your groomer, is going to continue grooming Freddie. She's using one of our vans until she purchases her own. She'll be contacting you personally to schedule appointments."

"I'm so relieved. Thank you for the years you groomed Freddy!" she gushed.

I gushed right back, "Thank you for your business!"

Another client, Mrs. Dixon, who suffered from multiple sclerosis and was totally dependent on us to take care of her shih tzu, Emily, also caught wind of the rumor.

When I picked up the phone, I could hear the panic in her voice. "Jan, it's not true, is it? Without you, I have no one to groom Emily. I tried some of those other mobile companies, but they just weren't as good with her as Rodney is. She gets so excited when he arrives, and I can depend on him to be here when he says he's going to. What am I going to do?"

"You'll be fine, Mrs. Dixon. Rodney is going to continue grooming Emily in one of our vans. In fact, he'll be starting his own business. He'll give you his business card and new number the next time he sees you."

"Oh, how wonderful; good for him! I hope you have a happy retirement, too, Jan."

Six months earlier, when Rodney had heard that Niel and I were pondering retirement, he had begun picking my brain each morning about how to run a business. He began arriving closer to 6:00, and on the morning that he got me out of bed, I scolded, "Rodney, I know you enjoy our morning chats, but this is way too early! No more arriving before 7:00."

The wisdom imparted in our early morning chats didn't travel in only one direction. Rodney educated me as much as I did him.

He suggested, "Say, since gas is skyrocketing, why don't you add on a surcharge until it comes down again?"

I wondered why I had simply grumbled about the climbing gas prices and not thought of that myself.

Another morning we brainstormed how to improve working conditions in the vans. "Have you thought about adding some big fans in the summer when we have to dry the dogs and turn the air conditioning off?"

Where was this man in the early years when I could really have used him, and how could I not have come up with that simple solution myself?

Rodney purchased our one, truly salvageable van that might—one thousand bucks later—pass inspection and be deemed roadworthy. He obtained the proper business licenses, and became successful in running his own mobile pet grooming business.

The transition went smoothly for all. It was a win-win situation for our groomers and for our clients. Wait—perhaps "all" was an exaggeration. We emerged with nary a nickel! When income didn't match out-go, we depleted our savings to pay bills and employees.

We sailed into our golden years without the gold. (Thank you, God, for Niel's government pension.) But we had many treasured memories—OK, that was a lie! Other than our wonderful pups, owners and a select few employees, the struggle to keep Canine Clippers afloat wasn't exactly filled with a multitude of joyous moments. If it had been, I wouldn't have continued to have nightmares about stalled vans and cranky dogs! In retrospect, it was easy to find humor in the outrageous, ridiculous incidents, but it wasn't so funny at the time.

There were rewards, of course. When I placed a well groomed pet into its owner's arms and heard, "Oh, he's never looked so good!" my ego soared, and I patted myself on the back for choosing this profession.

There was a lot to be said for those uplifting remarks. I clung to them on bad days and never tired of hearing them. At day's end, I had generally smiled more than frowned (very good for facial muscles).

Speaking of facials, here was another bonus: A by-product of working in a moist, warm environment was beautiful skin. Spending a day bent over warm water in a tub followed by blow-drying a wet dog was comparable to an hour in a sauna. When I heard, "Oh, you have such lovely skin" or even better, "You don't look your age," I smiled and told myself maybe, just maybe, it was worth it.

Other than a career as a personal trainer, where else could I spend an entire day exercising muscles, stretching tendons and bending knees while earning a living? Of course, the drawbacks were sore shoulders, torn rotator cuffs and cat bites on my neck that were difficult to explain to my significant other.

High on my list of bright points was my economical wardrobe. I never needed to keep up with the latest haute couture. Jeans or sweats with jaunty waterproof smocks worked well in winter. A switch to shorts in summer didn't require much thought when choosing my day's outfit. My clothing was so inexpensive that first year of operation, I forgot to include it as a tax deduction.

Did I mention the lack of boredom? My previous careers found me clock-watching. Not so with pet grooming. Time flew. The next customer and the next dog were always unique—each one an adventure. Plus, I wasn't working at a never-ending task with loose ends hanging over into the following day. Within an hour I arrived at a home, groomed a pet, collected my money and delivered a finished product—job done.

During the recession, in the 80s, we discovered that the downturning economy didn't have much effect on the pet grooming profession. Some customers scheduled their pet every six weeks instead of five, but we still had a waiting list, and none of our employees had to be laid off. Unlike purchasing a once-in-a-lifetime cemetery plot or providing a kidney transplant, pet grooming was a repeat customer trade. As my grooming instructor had told our class, "This is a bread and butter profession."

Twenty-one years earlier, when I revealed to my family that I was going to the dogs, my mother was right to question my judgment when she asked in astonishment, "You're going to do *what*?"

But if I had remained in my mind-numbing and premature-balding-causing civil service job, from where would the ammunition have come to write this book? You may even have recognized yourself or your pet as the *occasional* example of excellence. Or perhaps you were one of my terrific employees, especially if you stuck with me to the end. If so, thank you, and kudos for brightening my twenty-one years of "going to the dogs."

The biggest bonus? Not only did I still have a full head of hair, but I, too, snatched several of those straggly leftover grooming towels. Mom was right on about that. They did, indeed, make wonderful dust cloths!

Acknowledgments

· ·

Without the Gulf Coast Writers Association and the Florida Writers Association members sharing "what not to do," I would have spent three extra years making silly writing mistakes. I'm thankful that Piero Rivolta of New Chapter Publisher saw promise in my book and took a chance on this first-time author. Chris Angermann, Editor-in-Chief, encouraged me, and with his expert guidance, turned my raw material into an engaging, well-constructed story. Along with directing me to focus on "showing the journey," he walked me through the unfamiliar world of publishing. Thank you to Vanessa Houston, who did the final copy editing on the manuscript. Martha Jeffers, the "Grammar Granny," volunteered her editing expertise and never tired of correcting my German-influenced colloquialisms. Anita Dennis loyally reviewed chapters over and over and laughed at the appropriate places when I no longer viewed anything I wrote as humorous. Exactly at the right moments I heard, "You can do it girl," from AnnaLou Sonderman, Jane Sutton, Kathy Larsen, Brenda Stup, and Barbara Linthicum.

When monster computer problems plagued me, Tom Little generously spent hours, dropping whatever he was working on, to soothe the troubled beast. Along that same line, techies Annette Levesque-Nieman, Joan Jakobi and Fanci Shipp came to the rescue when I bawled, "I have a problem."

My optimistic mother, Esther, convinced me early in life that I could do anything, and I sure tried, although my pet grooming career threw her for a loop. Our daughter Kristin helped me to recall comical and horrific pet incidents that I had long since forgotten. Sons Mark, Scott, Jeff and David plugged in to offer support, but overall seemed awed that, rather than retiring, their mother was launching yet another career. My spouse Niel, as always and against his better judgment, joined my latest venture and provided me with a never-ending supply of ink cartridges, humor and love.

Lastly, when I couldn't quite fathom where God fit in with my new vocation, Pastor Jon Zehnder said, "The book is just the hook. Let your light shine." And I will.

**People wishing to contact Jan Nieman
can do so at:**

**www.authorjannieman.blogspot.com
nieman.jan7@gmail.com**